Investment Champions

Investment Champions

Richard Lander
A Citywire Publication

First published in Great Britain in 2005 by:
Citywire Financial Publishers Ltd,
1st Floor, 87 Vauxhall Walk, London SE11 5HJ.

ISBN 0-9546559-5-8

INVESTMENT NOTICE
Information provided in Investment Champions is for your general information and use. In particular, the information does not constitute any form
of specific advice or recommendation by Citywire Financial Publishers Ltd.
and is not intended to be relied upon by users in making (or refraining
from making) any investment decisions. Appropriate independent advice
should be obtained before making any such decision. Citywire Financial
Publishers will not be held liable for any errors, omissions or decisions
made on the basis of the information contained in this book.

Citywire Financial Publishers Ltd. is authorised and regulated by the
Financial Services Authority.

Author: Richard Lander

Executive Chairman: Lawrence Lever
Chief Executive: David Turner
Commercial Director: George Ball
Publishing Director: Sarah Landsberg
Director of Operations: Marion Hasson
Editor in Chief: Gavin Lumsden
Sub Editor: Andrew Freeman

Designed by Scratch Design (ag@scratchdesign.com)
Printed by Cambridge Printing

Contents

Contents

Citywire would like to thank the 10 fund management houses whose managers are featured in this book for their sponsorship of the individual chapters.

Foreword

This book will renew your faith in the power of the human touch.

Your car is built by robots in Poland, your bank's enquiry line is answered by an automated response system located in Azerbaijan and your coffee from the office drinks machine is untouched by human hand since the bean was picked off the bush in Guatemala.

By contrast, the billions of pounds of funds under management dealt with in Citywire's *Investment Champions* are all run by real people, and highly talented ones at that. These fund managers can make a huge difference to your future prosperity by picking the right stocks and bonds to invest in – and knowing which ones to avoid – and buying and selling them at the right time.

The next time someone suggests you by a fund picked by a computer, ask them whether they prefer a cup of freshly ground and brewed coffee or the instant stuff from the vending machine. The human touch will triumph every time.

Introduction

It is an interesting point to debate whether there has ever been a better time than today to be a fund manager or a more difficult time. It is quite easy to make persuasive cases for both sides of the argument.

Here is the case for the negative point of view. It is becoming much harder, in both equities and fixed-interest investments, to tell a good security from a bad one by its price.

Five years ago we had a stockmarket where favoured stocks traded at hefty multiples to their level of earnings, while those out of the limelight were bumping along with yields and earnings multiples both in the high single figures.

Yes, the market was completely out of whack because of its obsession with growth, technology and all things dotcom, but the prices were sending signals to investors, just as they are supposed to.

Today, multiples have been compressed to a much narrower range and the signals from stock prices are much less clear. We are no longer so obsessed with growth but realise that value and income are valid and necessary components to any equity portfolio.

It is the same in fixed-interest investments. Five years ago you paid a going rate for government bonds and a 10 percentage points premium or more for the privilege/thrill/risk of owning the paper issued by high-risk companies.

Today a wall of money coming into fixed interest has shrunk that margin by at least half. Some of the shrinkage is justified by the declining default rates of lowly-rated companies – but by no means all of it.

However, let's turn this argument on its head. The price of a stock or bond has always been the lazy investor's way of populating a portfolio. Anybody can read a price/earnings ratio in their morning newspaper or screen for this and a hundred other variables with a simple software program downloaded from the internet. If investment was just a case of picking the stocks with the right numbers attached to them we would all be millionaires.

But it was ever thus. When every rose in the garden looks much the same to the informed amateur, it takes a real expert to choose which one will turn out to be the prettiest.

In other words, brains and talent are back in fashion. In a world where ideas and cheap capital are in abundance, the ability to select a portfolio that will beat the market with an acceptable level of risk is the key quality that is scarce.

If the fund managers in this book share one thing it is possession of that very scarce talent. Each takes a very different approach to the market they operate in but all share the common trait of being able to look beyond the obvious for their portfolio choices.

No more is this the case than with the four fixed-interest investors featured in the book. Andrew Sutherland of Standard Life Investments has spent more than 20 years in the industry. Where once he dealt with picking straightforward debentures to match life and pension liabilities, he now runs or oversees a whole range of funds that cater for every type of investor, whatever their risk/reward profile. As anomalies become increasingly hard to find, Sutherland is pushing the Standard Life Investments fixed-interest operation to open up new frontiers to stay a step ahead of the competition.

In the same vein, Jonathan Platt and Sajiv Vaid at Royal London Asset Management are burning the midnight oil comparing one pub company's subordinated debentures with those of a rival firm. Okay, it may not be the most glamorous task in the investment world but it needs to be done and can bring vital rewards to investors. Just because a credit rating agency deems both sets of bonds to be A or B does not mean that shareholders will suffer the same penalties should the issuers default.

If you like life in the fast lane then have a look at the chapter on Mark Lieb, racing driver, winery owner and the world's leading investment manager in preferred securities. It is very likely that you know more about motor racing and wine making than these arcane securities which offer extra yield without the extra risk, in which case Lieb's story is well worth reading.

Among our eight equities managers we have three who are firmly placed in the value camp of the investment world. But all three have such different approaches to investing that you sometimes begin to doubt the (and please excuse the pun) value of labels such as value, growth and blend.

Of the three, perhaps Jens Moestrup Rasmussen, head of equities at Denmark's Sparinvest Fondsmaeglerselskab, is the most attached to the value concept. Rasmussen employs strict screening and numerical criteria to select stocks and to buy and sell them at the right time. Lest you get the impression from this that he is some kind of automaton who merely punches buy and sell orders, read on. Rasmussen knows the story behind every stock in his portfolio and shows great patience as that story plays out over periods of up to five years or more.

New York-based Rajiv Jain of Vontobel Asset Management shares some of Rasmussen's views in the way he approaches the market and in particular he has no time for what might be called 'The New, New Thing' that seems to excite some parts of the investment community, especially those who believe that business cycles are a thing of the past.

His overriding message – stick to your beliefs whatever is going on elsewhere. The past year has been testing for value investors but Jain is resolute. 'We had very little in energy or basic materials in the bull market but this is where execution gets difficult – you have to stick to your game plan,' he says.

The final value investor, Chris Burvill of Gartmore, shrugs his shoulder and smiles ruefully at all the former growth investors who like to attach the value label to their chests now that dividends are back in fashion. What Burvill cannot understand is why any UK equities investor bothered with growth at all when the London stockmarket has so few genuine large growth companies yet is chock-a-block with dividend-heavy, cash-rich value companies.

However, let's give growth a chance and again we have four managers all searching in places where the thundering herd of mainstream investors fail to look.

Europe, for example, is full of managers shouting and cursing at the backward economic policies of the EU's high and mighty. Not so Alex Darwall of Jupiter Asset Management for whom the sole criteria of selecting a company is that it is listed on a European stockmarket. Beyond that, they could be earning 90% of their profits by selling ice creams to Eskimos or (more likely) industrial gases to Taiwanese computer chip makers. There is, he says, much more to European companies than hobbled giants such as Fiat and Volkswagen.

Meanwhile over in Tokyo, David Mitchinson of JPMorgan Asset Management, is already an expert at uncovering hitherto ignored small and medium-sized companies on the Tokyo stockmarket where lack of analyst coverage has led to certain stocks being mispriced by 100% or more. Having moved to Tokyo a year ago, Mitchinson has hit the ground running as the economy, consumer confidence and corporate restructuring all show positive trends.

Our last investors are UK specialists but with a twist. Ted Scott of F&C Asset Management has earned his spurs running ethical funds which give him the difficult task of choosing his portfolio from a very short list handed to him by two ethical screening committees. He has underlined his native talent this year by taking over a non-ethical fund and giving it a new lease of life.

Last but not least are Jan Luthman and Stephen Bailey of Walker Crips Weddle Beck who see investment through the world in which we live. They spend much of their time identifying top-down themes and

strive to build a portfolio that is in harmony with national and international economic, political and social influences such as ageing populations, globalisation and global warming.

So this is our selection of Investment Champions for 2006. Not only
are they profoundly good fund managers, but they are all interesting
people who think deeply about the investments they make and the
environment in which they make them.

They know that investment is a serious business because at the end
of the chain – directly or indirectly – someone is lending them a stack
of hard-earned money and they would dearly like it to be larger by the
time they get it back.

My guess is that if you asked these 12 managers whether or not this
is a good time to be a fund manager, they would also say yes without
hesitation.

But then they are among the most talented in the field, so they do
have something of an unfair advantage.

Steady earner

Chris Burvill,

Gartmore

by Richard Lander

Why do buses always travel in packs of three? What is the meaning of life? And why are there no very large growth companies listed on the London Stock Exchange?

Don't bother asking Chris Burvill for the answers to questions one and two – he is a fund manager, for goodness sake, not a professor of philosophy. However, he is pretty strong when it comes to question three, as befits a manager whose approach to investment has worked extremely well over a period of almost 20 years.

Burvill has worked for the last three years at Gartmore, where he runs two funds – the £260 million UK Equity Income fund, managed jointly with Brian Gallagher and the £250 million Cautious Managed fund where he can juggle the balance of assets in the fund between equities, bonds and cash.

Having started running equity income funds at Commercial Union in 1987, Burvill spent 10 years working for Guinness Flight (which later became Investec) where he started a remarkable run of beating the average manager in the Cautious Managed sector for five years in succession.

Value-based equity income investing is what Burvill has excelled at during those 18 years, although it was a part of the market he entered almost by accident. 'I got the high yield equity sectors such as financial and retail when I was an analyst at Commercial Union,' he says.

'All the racy sectors had been taken by other people on the team and there was nobody else left to do the job. Had I not volunteered to cover them then I would have been given them anyway.'

Despite having income investing thrust upon him, rather than being born into it, there is no doubt that Burvill is temperamentally suited to stories that stress consistency and steady growth prospects than ones that claim to have invented The Next Big Thing. Were he a fisherman, Burvill would demand to see what is in your net rather than take as gospel your fishy tales about just how big the one that got away was.

Growing pains

'To be an equity income investor you will naturally struggle with any story about momentum while anything to do with 'blue sky' growth will also be unpalatable' he says. 'You are very likely to be a contrarian who is cynical about a particular company's prospects.'

Burvill says he has often tried to answer the question about why big growth companies have such a small presence among the higher echelons of the FTSE 100 constituents. After all, London is one of the world's biggest and most open capital markets, with huge sums of cash available to fund expansion at all stages of a company's life cycle.

But while the leader board of the New York Stock Exchange features mature growth companies such as Microsoft, IBM and Cisco, the UK has ... well, we have Tesco and that's just about it.

'There is a certain irony about Tesco because it comes from the food retailing sector rather than something more growth-based like telecoms or technology,' he says. 'But it is the only true growth stock among the largest 10 in London – the rest of them [companies such as BP, Royal Bank of Scotland and Vodafone] have all got to where they are today through acquisition.'

One of the primary reasons Burvill thinks that this has come about is the undue pressure to find growth asserted by UK investors. 'They are desperate to get into growth and that means that companies which are labelled growth stories are just as desperate not to disappoint their hopes and dreams,' he says.

'The result is that they then take a short cut to growth by funding acquisitions which very often go wrong, because they undertake them too early and too quickly to respond to this pressure,' he says. 'Organic growth (per se) is absolutely fine but it never tends to happen in the way that you would like.'

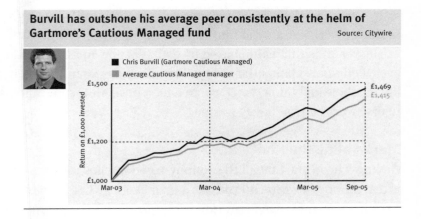

Burvill has outshone his average peer consistently at the helm of Gartmore's Cautious Managed fund
Source: Citywire

As an example, he cites the telecoms sector and in particular the mobile market. Growth in usage has been spectacular over the past five years but your investment in Vodafone would have declined by more than 40% over that period as it scooped up foreign acquisitions costing more than £130 billion and then wrote their value down in double quick order.

In other words, great company, lousy investment. 'The rise of Vodafone is a remarkable achievement,' wrote leading economist John Kay at the height of its buying frenzy. 'But no special business insight is needed to buy assets for far more than they are worth.'

So Chris Burvill is a value man but as he says, we are all value investors now. Five years ago, the equities market had a spectacular range of ratings for investors to choose from.

Growth investors could head for companies with price/earnings ratios of 30 or higher if they believed their stories of greater things to come, while value investors had their pick of companies whose dividend yields exceeded their earnings multiples.

Today multiples are far more compressed and Burvill thinks it is a result of the equity income approach proving its worth. 'Equity income has given investors everything they could have asked for – share price performance and growing income, all seemingly with much lower risk than you find elsewhere,' he says.

'The result is that value-based investing is now incredibly popular – everybody now claims they are value investing. So if we are all looking for the same thing, you have to look a little bit further and deeper to discover the true keys to value.'

Marks of distinction

Having a head start on all the Johnny-come-latelies in value investing is a great help for Burvill who has a firm idea of what he likes and dislikes in companies. One criterion is that he likes to invest in businesses that really make a difference to the world around us by making a useful product or providing a useful service to its customers.

'I struggle with investing in companies that make a business out of arbitrage or trading something,' he says. 'I want a company that its customers would miss if it was not around.'

One example of this type of company is Rolls-Royce. 'Rolls is one of only two major aero engine manufacturers in the world today,' he says. 'If it was not around then General Electric would have a monopoly on supplying engines to the aircraft makers and flying would be very much more expensive for all of us.' In other words, a Rolls-Royce less world would be noticed by everyone taking a cheap weekend away on one the UK's budget airlines.

Burvill is also intrigued by the customer loyalty that a brand can command even when the company is not having a very good time of it. Marks & Spencer was on its uppers a short while ago, shunned, it was said, both by women of a certain age and those a great deal younger who saw their fashions as tatty and dowdy.

But while other investors followed the shoppers to the door marked exit, what struck Burvill was that sales were incredibly resilient.

True, turnover was hardly increasing but, by holding steady at £8 billion a year, it dispelled the image that nobody was shopping at M&S anymore.

CV

Born: 15 July 1958
Career: Burvill was appointed to Gartmore in December 2002 as head of UK Equity Income. He started out as a management trainee with National Mutual of Australia before joining Commercial Union as a UK equities investment analyst. He managed the CU Income fund from 1987 to 1990 before embarking on a 10-year stint at Guinness Flight, which later became Investec.

'That steadiness said to me that not only were many of its customers loyal, but if they got their fashions right, sales had every opportunity to improve,' he said. The hunch paid off when retailer extraordinaire Philip Green launched his takeover bid, the shares soared and Burvill, in his own words, 'made some very decent money'.

The intellectual property of a company is also a factor that sets things fluttering on Burvill's radar screen. Intangible assets on a balance sheet are one thing, but Burvill wants to unearth something in the company's real business that you cannot assign numbers to. 'My idea of intellectual property value is something that you cannot really measure but it is definitely a factor to look for,' he says. 'I want to see an idea or product that is significantly differentiated and has patent protection or a significant barrier to entry and which customers really need,' he says.

Burvill is not really a top-down sort of investor. He admits that his work does have a macro-economic edge to it but such analysis is secondary to his preference for evaluating his investments one company at a time. For example, he feels that a top-down view of the telecoms sector would probably lead a rational investor to avoid it given its heavy capital expenditure demands, intense competition and high level of scrutiny from national and international regulatory bodies.

INVESTMENT STRATEGY

- Takes account of macro-economic factors but prefers to evaluate stocks on a company-by-company basis and meets at least 200 businesses a year
- Has clear ideas about the type of companies he wants to invest in and will search out firms that provide useful products or services, or those that are significantly different from the competition
- Responds to the changing tides of investor sentiment and its influence on the stockmarket

---

However, the merits are there on a company-by-company basis. Burvill highlights the case of BT Group. Taken as a whole, national incumbent landline telephone companies have little to commend them as nimbler rivals take market share away. Burvill admits that at the top line, BT is going nowhere fast – it has gone ex-growth. The attraction, however, is what is going on at each line below.

'Gross profits are marching ahead very strongly because of the company's extensive cost-cutting [BT employed almost 137,000 people in 2000 but now has just 102,000 on its payroll] while the investment in its new 21st century network should make the company considerably more efficient and profitable,' he says.

Burvill also thinks BT will be in line for a welcome and substantial reduction in its borrowing costs in the near future.

'The company had to refinance at high interest rates a few years ago. Most of those terms will drop off in the next three years and the company should be able to refinance at much lower interest rates,' he says. 'So at the bottom line we can see if the lower gearing will lead to either higher dividends or share buybacks. It is the ideal situation for our sort of fund.'

No slave to dividends

For an equity income manager, Burvill is remarkably insouciant about dividend yields in his portfolio. The ground rules for his Equity Income fund says that it must yield overall at least 10% above the average market yield after costs.

With the benchmark so low at 3.1%, the task to surpass it is not overly burdensome according to Burvill. 'It is simple maths really – if the market was yielding 5% on average, it would be a much tougher task holding lower yielding shares,' he says.

His attitudes to dividend levels have changed over the years in line with the way companies and investors see them today. 'There are plenty of good quality stocks around today yielding 5-6%. We are always aware of yields but for me they have tended to take a more secondary role in the way I have valued stocks over the past five years,' he says.

Ten years ago, holding a dividend intact was an act of faith by a company to its investors and it would do its utmost to maintain its payments in the bad times. BP famously once raised a rights issue from its shareholders which it essentially returned to them as a dividend.

'This would underpin share prices if things went wrong,' says Burvill. 'But today things have changed a great deal. Companies are much more willing to cut dividends in difficult times; that means that yield is no longer quite the arbiter that it was in the past.'

Today Burvill says he likes to rely more on other financial indicators such as a company's price to book ratio, price/earnings or earnings before interest – and he is quite happy to hold companies that do not pay a dividend if he believes them to be undervalued.

Small talk

Unusually perhaps for a value investor, Burvill has no great affinity for the smaller company sector and holds a very minor proportion of his equity income portfolio in the bottom end of the market. He reckons that, when running a retail unit trust, you might as well go for larger companies unless their respective valuations make the case for a smaller company or it offers a very specialised set of goods or services that larger companies cannot match.

He does hold a few of these smaller gems that pass these tests. One such company is ATH, an open cast coal mining business in Scotland which Burvill reckons has strong prospects as more nuclear plants are decommissioned and further calls are made for imported gas.

Another smaller pick is the computer services group Civica, which provides highly-specialised consulting, software and managed services to the public sector and which Burvill describes as: 'An example of a niche where a smaller company can produce better returns than a larger one.'

Whatever size of stocks that he picks for his portfolio, Burvill is fully aware that there is no point in picking a company that might be brilliant at what it does if rather more investors are selling the shares than are buying it and the investment loses money.

From this perspective, Burvill shares the view of the legendary economist John Maynard Keynes who was a fairly crafty investor himself, making piles of money both for himself and King's College Cambridge where he held the position of bursar. Keynes compared getting things right in the stockmarket with betting on the winner of a beauty contest.

Writing his famous treatise *The General Theory of Employment, Interest and Money*, Keynes opined that: 'It is not a case of choosing those [faces] which, to the best of one's judgment, are really the prettiest, nor even those which average opinion genuinely thinks the prettiest ... we devote our intelligences to anticipating what average opinion expects the average opinion to be.'

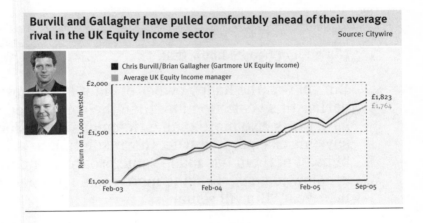

Burvill and Gallagher have pulled comfortably ahead of their average rival in the UK Equity Income sector   Source: Citywire

Or, as Burvill puts it more succinctly: 'Most returns for investors come through a re-rating of a company rather than any actual change in the company itself.' In other words, anticipate that a company will be re-rated upwards by the rest of the market, get in there first and reap the rewards.

That is precisely what Burvill did with cigarette group British American Tobacco (BAT) five years ago when it traded on six times earnings. The shares were dirt cheap and virtually discounting the very remote possibility that the company would go down under a tonne of health-related litigation.

Today BAT is pretty much the same company it was in 2000 but perception has changed to the point where the shares now stand on 14 times earnings – far too high in Burvill's opinion.

It is this kind of insight which Burvill reckons gives him and other good fund managers the edge over the City's stockbroking analysts who can tell you every last detail about the global tobacco industry – from the state of the crop in Kentucky to impending public area legislation across the European Union and BAT's place in the grander scheme of things – but still come to the wrong conclusion about the shares.

Not a lot of people know that:

Burvill was the happy owner of eight lawn-mowers earlier this year. 'No more than the garden needs,' says Chris. 'No more than a ridiculous obsession,' says his exasperated wife. Her resolution to get rid of most of them has made some progress and there are now just six. 'Leaving more room for a new one next year,' Burvill remarks.

'What they fail to do consistently is to see the wood for the trees,' he says. 'They do all the hard work but don't concentrate on how investors will react to the figure they have worked out. It's not their area of speciality and not what they are paid to do.'

What Burvill does is continuously talk to anybody he can lay his hands on if he thinks they can help confirm or challenge his ideas about a stock. He likes to meet the companies themselves – he reckons he gets to see at least 200 a year – and to discuss what he finds out about them with Gartmore's ranks of analysts and fund managers.

He also keeps a lively dialogue going with a coterie of around 10 brokers in City investment banks who he has got to know and trust over the past decades and who act as both foils for his views and generators of new investment ideas.

That discourse seems likely to keep going for a while yet. Burvill's ambition is to build up his equity income fund to be one the larger players in its sector and reckons he might just do that. 'We have a lot going for us and there is a great need for this type of fund,' he says.

Even if he did want to do something else, he is not terribly confident that he would pull it off. 'I would struggle badly not doing this job,' he says, although he admits to being a reasonably good pianist who would benefit greatly from extra time practising at the keyboard. Music's loss for the moment is the income investor's gain.

In good company

Alex Darwall,

Jupiter Asset Management

by Richard Lander

Alex Darwall has a straightforward approach to running money for his clients who want to invest in European equities. His philosophy is focus on the companies that are most likely to succeed, leave the politics to the politicians and asset allocation to the asset allocators.

'As far as I'm concerned it is one market out there,' he says. 'They are just companies. Of course I know which stockmarkets they are listed on but it hardly matters these days where a lot of them are based.'

In other words – concentrate on the companies, get that right and you won't do too badly. The formula may not be complex – and may disappoint those who see rocket science as a necessary part of modern fund management – but it is one that has worked well enough for Darwall who has built up a strong reputation as a European specialist in the 10 years he has worked for Jupiter Asset Management.

Formerly an analyst with a background in French equities at de Zoete & Bevan and Goldman Sachs, he has been in charge of his present vehicle, the £1 billion Jupiter European fund, since January 2001.

A firm approach
Darwall's proposition is that he invests in European companies and emphatically not Europe or its singular approach to business, its

dreams of political unification or its many and varied cultural tastes.

There is a big difference and Darwall has some strong words for those who confuse such matters.

'Asset allocators have been very negative on Europe because of the political breakdown that we have seen over the past year. I can totally understand their reasons, but the companies I invest in have nothing to do with politics,' he says.

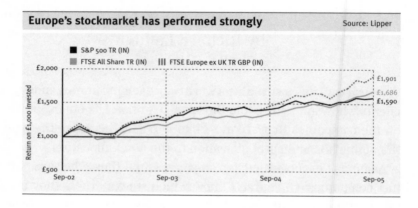

Europe's stockmarket has performed strongly — Source: Lipper

'So we have the situation where the asset allocators have been sceptical yet the markets have been among the best performing in the world. They just got things wrong.' Taking things further, Darwall reckons the traditional asset allocation approach which says something like 'we must be overweight here and underweight there' has been left behind. Today the world economy is much more unified through overseas ownership of companies and outsourcing of production and services.

But it would be unfair just to heap blame on the asset allocators. If they have been negative on Europe in recent years it is because they have seen how badly the politicians of the Continent (let's cut to the quick – the European Union) have faltered and seen their grandiose dreams of an overarching constitution come crashing around them.

The denouement came in 2005 when both France and the Netherlands rejected the new proposed EU constitution.

'It's all failed,' says Darwall who would place himself firmly in the Eurosceptic camp of the political divide. Again, his answer is simple: don't let politics get in the way of a good investment story.

No-go areas

As he admits, politics do interfere with the fortunes of many companies in Europe, directly, or indirectly and these are the businesses that need to be avoided. Companies to be shunned for being indirect victims of EU politics include the retailers of France and Germany where consumer confidence has been crushed within an inch of its life by economic and social policies that have created high levels of unemployment.

The more overt victims of political interference include companies that Darwall steers well clear of. 'VW and Daimler are examples of companies which suffer political pressure because politicians see them as national champions. It is the same story in France where the state wants to protect what they see as key companies,' he says.

'The companies I invest in have nothing to do with politics,' says Darwall. Speaking just before the German elections in September 2005, he said the outcome would be largely irrelevant to any company in his portfolio. Just as well really as the deadlocked outcome promised weeks and possibly months of uncertainty for the country's governance.

The world has moved on and while Darwall accepts the stricture of his fund that he must invest in European-listed companies, he prefers to take a one-world perspective; geography is almost irrelevant today.

World class

Darwall throws down a challenge. 'With most companies in which I invest I could hide the name in the transcripts of our conversation, and you could not guess which country they are based in – or even if they come from Europe.'

'The good companies that I meet don't mention how the economic problems of Europe will affect their business. And if they do mention it, they generally refer to it with the same emphasis as what is going on in the US and China,' he adds.

What genuinely impresses Darwall is the ability of the best European companies to take advantage of modern technology to expand their operations overseas. 'You can now get companies operating all over the world in ways they could never do before,' he says. 'Instant communication means they can develop software there and operate from Europe with amazing control of a local office. You can video conference with employees there and even change their swipe cards from over here.'

All this is made more effective by the almost complete breakdown in barriers to get the right people doing the right things in the right places. Darwall speaks with some awe of meeting people of Indian origin controlling businesses in the US on behalf of European companies.

This international traffic of people and services is in Darwall's view, perversely encouraged by the litany of labour and business regulations that puts off so many investors from taking European equities seriously as an asset class.

'If you are a company in France or Germany coping with a difficult social and economic backdrop, then you are encouraged to develop overseas – you have to do it to grow,' he says. 'Necessity is the mother of invention and some companies have done it very well.

'By contrast the ones that stay behind enjoying the protection of national barriers will be in big trouble one day when that protection finally comes down. Besides it engenders a culture of complacency.' Darwall reckons that European companies are often rather better than their American counterparts at taking their skills overseas. In many cases, they have been there for far longer, charging behind their countries' governments in the rather less than glorious imperialist escapades that carved up much of Africa, the Middle East and Asia in the early part of the last century.

'You see companies such as Unilever who are far bigger in Africa and have far deeper roots than their American rivals. The French have certain advantages in the Middle East and China, the Dutch ties in Indonesia go back many years, while Spain and Portugal have strong historic links to Latin America,' he says.

CV

Born: 13 June 1963
Career: Darwall started out as an analyst with Zoete & Bevan (BZW) and in 1987 moved to Paris to front the French equity research division at Swedish group Enskilda Securities. In 1992 he joined Goldman Sachs as a French equity analyst before Jupiter snapped him up in 1995. In 1999 he was given control of the Jupiter European investment trust and subsequently the roll-over vehicle, the Jupiter European Opportunities Trust. He was appointed fund manager for the Jupiter European fund in 2001.

Some global companies such as Unilever may be household names from the Cape to Cairo but other European companies striding the world stage that Darwall cites would mean little to most consumers. One of his biggest holdings in his European fund is Novozymes, a Danish business that took the output from the Carlsberg fermentation process and is now, well, probably the best industrial enzyme company in the world.

'This is a company that has a 44% share of its market in the world – you don't have to look at it for very long to work out that it did not get that big from operating in Denmark,' says Darwall. The state of the

Danish economy, and the fortunes of its beer, butter and bacon industries on its budget deficit or balance of payments are irrelevant as far as Darwall is concerned. Similarly, even the hobbled, stifled and terminally bureaucratic economy of France manages to throw up some global leaders that can hold their position with the best despite, rather than because of, the policies that emerge from the Elysée Palace.

'You have a company like Dassault Systemes which makes the best computer aided design and manufacturing systems (CAD/CAM) in the world with a customer list that includes Boeing and Toyota – the undoubted leaders in their respective industries.

'Or you have Air Liquide, another French based company that is everywhere including being number one in China. What matters to them is not so much the direction of French retail consumption but a whole series of other factors such as the state of the semiconductor sector in Taiwan where they sell their industrial gases.

Focal points

Darwall has more impressive companies to reel off from his portfolio but is unapologetic that the list is a short one – around 35-40 companies account for the £1 billion he has under his control. 'We focus on companies that meet certain criteria, where we have got a good understanding and where we think we can spot something that other people have not yet found.

'But it is a pretty short list because the market as a whole is rather smart and by and large there are not many companies where I can say "I feel I have an edge".'

Darwall also likes to take a sword to the Aunt Sally that a small portfolio is a risky one. 'A concentrated portfolio is a lot less risky than a large one. A big portfolio means that you are diluting your good ideas with weaker ones and companies that you know less about,' he says.

He argues that the Jupiter European fund is made up of a chain of single companies with risks that are unconnected with each other and not dependent on a particular economic scenario.

Darwall sleeps easy even though he has at times 9% or more in a single stock. 'Yes of course it would hurt me if Neopost [the French mail-room equipment and logistics systems group which was his biggest holding in late 2005] went bust tomorrow.

'In any case the effect is just the same as someone losing 0.5% in 18 stocks they hold on the same day. My degree of confidence in what I own leads me to have a concentrated portfolio built like this,' he says.

Getting down to business

That confidence stems from what he believes is a really thorough understanding of the companies he owns – and he stresses this is a personal affair. 'What I think I do after 20 years in this business is to understand just how these companies make money. That means reading the report and accounts, meeting the companies and coming up with our own opinions,' he says.

INVESTMENT STRATEGY

- Avoids politics and asset allocation in favour of a bottom-up strategy which places the company centre stage
- Prefers businesses which have a global outlook that are able to expand their operations overseas
- Runs a concentrated portfolio of 35-40 stocks
- A firm's discounted cashflow is the key valuation measure

He uses analysts' reports sparingly. His time is better spent (as an ex-analyst) meeting companies. Besides, he says: 'You end up not analysing the companies but analysing the analyst and that is a totally different set of skills.'

Sticking to the company rather than the market has stood Darwall in good stead throughout the almost unprecedented volatility of the last 10 years.

'It means that I didn't get sucked in to the internet bubble. You get to avoid the joy and panic of the herd.'

After the initial stage of understanding the company, Darwall likes to ask himself whether its businesses can improve their standing in the world. If the answer to this is positive, the final criterion for a company to enter the Darwall portfolio is valuation – in other words 'how much would we pay compared with the current market price?'

Typically, Darwall selects companies whose success tends to depend above all on their own efforts. He tries to identify certain 'winning' characteristics in companies across all sectors. This involves stripping away the ephemeral factors and focusing on the key drivers and attributes of that company. The aim is to spot companies with structural, sustainable advantages which that company can leverage to grow earnings at an above-average rate.

Not a lot of people know that:

Darwall enjoys keeping fit by playing the sport of kings – and we're not talking horse racing but Real Tennis, as enjoyed by that famous Tudor Henry VIII, among others.

By cross-checking this analysis with a 'sanity check' (in effect, seeing if it looks reasonable in the context of his investment experience) the hope is to construct a good quality portfolio.

He also tries to see if there is a catalyst – technological, regulatory and so forth – which is helping a company exploit its advantages better and faster. The investment process tries to minimise the impact of 'macro' factors which are beyond the influence of that company, factors that are notoriously hard to analyse.

The object of this process is to make better quality investment decisions: lower risk for better reward. This, allied to due patience, produces consistent outperformance.

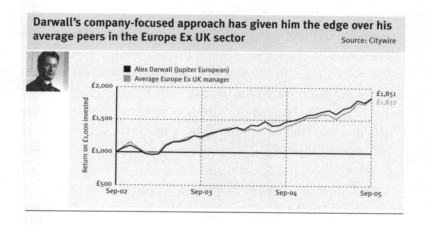

Darwall's company-focused approach has given him the edge over his average peers in the Europe Ex UK sector   Source: Citywire

When it comes to valuation, Darwall relies on calculating a business's discounted cashflow – in other words a projection of how much money a company will throw off year by year, calculated in present-day terms and taking into account factors such as the level of interest rates and risk.

'Discounted cashflow gives you a measure of the return you get from a firm's assets. But discounted cashflow gives you a picture of real cash and real profits projected forward in a stream of earnings.'

If that sounds like a cast iron numerical formula, Darwall is keen to avoid the impression that he treats portfolio construction as a mathematical science rather than an art. Instead Darwall's experience of what companies do right and wrong over time plays a valuable role.

Tales of the unexpected

Portfolio choices can and do go wrong. 'Nothing is ever a perfect investment and there always has to be an element of compromise in the stocks you choose. I can make what appear to be perfectly reasonable investment choices but what happens is the company fails to deliver as I expected it would,' he said.

Again, analysis is the key to a better portfolio – learn and move on. 'It tends to be the case that my mistakes happen because despite very good evidence that a company has delivered in the past, has good management and a strong record, things change,' he says.

'You have to accept the fact that while there are tremendous opportunities out there, you can be mistaken in your reasonable assumptions. It might be the case that the market where a company operates reacts in a way that we simply didn't expect. For example, a company's sales projections might be completely upset if rivals come in with totally irrational pricing policies.'

Above all it is a time-consuming business that can eat the soul. 'Investment consumes a lot of energy. The turnover of my portfolio is certainly lower than the average but that does not prevent the need to be thinking about what is going on all the time to avoid any hint of complacency. I am very vigilant in the way I run my investments and that can be very demanding.'

Much of that energy is consumed at Jupiter's headquarters on London's Hyde Park Corner where Darwall meets two or three companies every day. Much as he likes Europe as a leisure destination, he seldom goes to see companies there. 'It really would be a very bad use of my time. If a chief executive officer (CEO) of a European company comes to our offices I can get his full and undivided attention,' he says.

'If he or she is not prepared to come to London to meet us then it is probably a strong indication that the firm in question is not terribly interested in the fate of minority shareholders.' One such company's CEO who could not find the time or the air fare to make it to London was Parmalat, the Italian food conglomerate. That delivered the message to Darwall that he should avoid the stock, well before the small matter of a £10 billion hole in the financial accounts appeared in 2003.

The long and the short of it

Darwall has no burning ambition to widen his net – the European fund and its investment trust cousin, the Jupiter European Opportunities Trust, are more than enough to fill his plate. While there are Jupiter colleagues who successfully combine both long only and long/short investments, Darwall has no desire at all to run a hedge fund.

'Long-only suits me much better,' he says. 'I really do enjoy meeting talented people who run very good companies. There is a satisfaction in following and understanding a company that develops successfully over time. It's a very satisfying way to make money.

'You need a completely different mindset for a long/short fund and even in long-only I don't think I could run different value and growth funds,' he says.

Darwall likes Jupiter and its investor-oriented style of fund management. 'You have a nice balance here of an enterprise culture and the resources that allow me to get on with the job. My investment approach is appreciated here because I can have the freedom to do what I want and there are resources to take care of things like compliance.'

Darwall talks of the need to work at a certain rhythm with the right amount of patience. It is a tough balancing act but one he seems to be getting right most of the time – in stark contrast to what the great and the good at the top of the European Union manage to do at any time.

Less is more

Rajiv Jain,
Vontobel Asset Management, Inc.,
New York

by Richard Lander

There are two ways to go about running an international equities asset management operation. The first involves building an army of analysts and portfolio managers around the world in the belief that might is right and having people on the ground and close to the action will give you a competitive advantage over your rivals.

The other way is to take the view that small is beautiful and that in a world where communications and information retrieval is instant, what you really need is a small group of very smart people who could just as well be situated in a small town or New York.

Actually, let's go for New York – it's more fun and you are more likely to persuade companies to come and visit you there. The other reason for choosing the Big Apple is that is where Rajiv Jain heads up a small team to run the global equity value portfolios for Vontobel Asset Management, Inc., a wholly-owned subsidiary of Vontobel Holding AG, the international Swiss banking and investment group.

Jain is a firm believer in the less is more view when it comes to running investment funds. 'Smaller teams tend to be more focused and cohesive than having dozens of analysts,' he says. But he admits that there are plenty of others who disagree with that point of view.

'People often want the comfort of seeing wall maps of the world with pins stuck in all over it,' he says.

Indeed, it was a view that held some sway within Vontobel at one time as the group decided to outsource the Vontobel Fund - Far East Equity to a Singapore-based asset management team.

The $1.5 billion fund (30 September) has achieved quite a lot since moving back within Jain's domain, as have the other funds he has been responsible for, covering the emerging markets, Europe and global (ex-US). All have tended to consistently outperform their benchmarks by a healthy margin (400 to 500 basis points per year) as their portfolios become more progressively influenced by Jain and his team's value investment philosophy.

A value investor with a difference

Jain is a value investor but is a very different species from the extreme members of that fraternity who can sometimes take a fire and brimstone view of the investment world in which any deviation from the value mantra is sacrilege. Yes, Jain sticks to many of the familiar value mantras – read Warren Buffett, buy cheap and sell according to your head, not your heart.

So far, so classic. But on several counts, Jain deviates from the party line. For him value stocks are not the clearly identifiable species that some define them as. Many in his portfolio could also be classified as having growth credentials while at the same time he does not regard value as a synonym for 'burnt out stock'.

'The difference between a value and growth stock is a lot more superficial that many people in the market like to believe,' he says. As an example he takes the case of Tesco, the British supermarket empire which has achieved astonishing success at home and abroad in recent years.

'Tesco trades on a price/earnings multiple of about 13 times at the moment – does that make it a value stock or a growth company? It is the same if you take a look at Kensington [another UK company which offers mortgages to what are known as sub-prime lenders – the ones traditional lenders prefer to avoid]. This company is on an earnings multiple of 7 but has grown at 20% a year over the past three years. Can you tell me whether that is value or growth?

'The point is that value comes from the growth that a company has to deliver and both types of investors want to pay less than the company is worth. We look for growth businesses at discounted prices.'

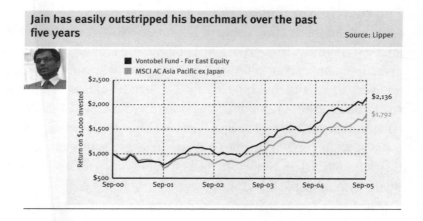

Jain has easily outstripped his benchmark over the past five years

Source: Lipper

Nor is he mechanistic in his approach – he will take the time to evaluate the potential of a stock even if it hasn't managed to jump the statistical barriers normally required to make it into one of his portfolios. 'Many people want a cookie cutter system when it comes to asset management,' he says. 'But it is not a 100% science – it has an element of art in it as well.'

Most engagingly, Jain does not portray himself as an investment super hero who got it all right when the rest of us got it all badly wrong. He has grown into value investing rather than being born into the faith, and in doing so has learned from the mistakes he has made along the way.

'You learn a lot more in bear markets than in the bull rallies – as in life generally, you get more wisdom when you struggle,' he says. 'You think you know a lot but you realise you don't know that much and you come out the other end being a lot more realistic and humble.

'Looking back I would probably do some things differently today but on the other hand I am just glad that I worked through the big bear market when I was relatively young.'

The road to Vontobel

Jain took an interesting route to Vontobel's New York office which he joined in 1994. His first experience of handling money was as a currency hedge manager for a large Indian textiles firm which did business all over Asia – a period he described as invaluable experience for the road ahead. He then joined some friends to manage a small private trust in Florida and ended up taking an MBA in the sunshine state.

His first major job in the equities business came when he joined Swiss Bank Corp in New York as a global equities analyst – a move he made with inauspicious timing.

'SBC had just taken over Brinson Partners [A Chicago-based money management firm with, coincidentally, value underpinnings] and they were looking to move everyone to the mid west,' he said. Preferring the Big Apple to the Windy City, Jain jumped ship to Vontobel at the invitation of an ex-SBC colleague.

The value drive emerged from Jain's first job at Vontobel which was to develop the screening process then used to select portfolio stocks. A combined top-down/bottom-up, highly quantitative model, the process soon struck Jain as being less than watertight at times of extreme stress, two of which – the Russian debt crisis and collapse of most of Asia's currencies – blighted the financial markets during the late 1990s.

'I realised at that time that the top-down approach was not as effective as I thought. There always seemed to be a new reason why the emerging markets were turning nasty,' he says. 'At the same time, most of the European countries were aligning with each other as they prepared for monetary union, so what was the top-down purpose there?

Kindred spirits

Jain also started to read the legendary annual reports of Berkshire Hathaway, the investment company chaired by the greatest value investor of all, Warren Buffett. Light years away from the conventional annual reports that line a million cat trays around the world, the Berkshire Hathaway tome contains Buffett's reflections on the year just gone and his value-driven views of what he thinks is about to unfold.

CV

Born: 27 January 1968
Career: Jain's 16 years' investment experience began with Swiss Bank Corp, now UBS, where he held a portfolio management position. He joined Vontobel Asset Management, Inc. in 1994 and now holds the titles of managing director and senior vice president. He is senior portfolio manager for Vontobel's international value equity portfolios, overseeing the research effort and portfolio construction.

'I started reading the reports and it was not so much a case of a light going on immediately as making me start thinking about how they applied to what I did,' said Jain. As he started applying the Buffett philosophy, it reaffirmed his own ideas about going for quality stocks for his emerging markets portfolio, the first fund to which he applied the Buffett ideals. 'I always tended that way but reading Buffett reinforced me. So we had nothing in the Russian bull market of 1996 and nothing when the market collapsed in 1999,' he says.

Under pressure

The late 1990s were a testing time to apply value principles. 'The technology bubble of 1999 meant we didn't do well that year – in fact things couldn't have been worse. But at least the lessons we were learning were being tested immediately and were working. As Buffett says: "If principles don't stand the test of time then they are not principles."

As the bubble burst there was clear evidence that the downside of growth investing was far more painful than underperforming a rally. The Vontobel Fund - Global Value Equity (ex US) was affected strongly at the time as it was not managed according to today's value principles.

'The fund bought a lot of high-multiple growth stocks especially in Japan,' Jain says. 'We thought that they were cheap at 30 times earnings and expected them to go to 40 times.' The irony was that these equities ended up trading at around 100 times earnings – not, alas, because the share prices had soared but because earnings had collapsed as the Japanese economy went into almost total meltdown.

Quality control

The value investment process that Jain and his team members have built at Vontobel Asset Management, Inc. is centred on quality rather than finding a collection of beaten-up stocks that the market has somehow overlooked. Instead he wants to find companies that in his words, have delivered in the past but are for some reason not doing that well at the current time.

'You have to try to buy a business not a stock and then value the stock like a business. We don't want turnaround or restructuring stories but we want to find a company where the returns on equity should be reasonable. We are not asking for 15% a year but we do like at least 10% without too much leverage.'

As Jain admits, sifting for stocks with these criteria can limit the scope of the search. Indeed in some countries the cupboard can be completely bare. However, Jain takes such situations in his stride.

'Our Vontobel Fund - European Value Equity had nothing in either Germany or France that was good enough for us for a couple of years, while the Vontobel Fund - Global Value Equity has around 6.5-7% in Japan against an index weighting of around 25%. The companies we like are too expensive while the rest are mediocre businesses.'

Not a lot of people know that:

Jain has most of his personal wealth invested in the Vontobel funds he manages– a big vote of confidence from the man that counts.

This is one reason why Vontobel's international value funds have concentrated portfolios. At any given time the four funds might have around 105-110 stocks between them. The other reason is that Jain has very little truck with the perception that a more diversified portfolio is a less risky one. 'Ten stocks in a fund may be risky but once you get to 30 names the risks should have gone. If you understand those 30 stocks then the risk is less rather than more,' he says.

At one level, Jain points out, diversification comes easily in mandates as widespread as the ones he runs. 'We have about 50 names in the Vontobel Fund - Far East Equity in a dozen countries, and it should be very clear that an Australian food retailer has very little in common with a Korean food retailer,' he says.

Single-minded

However, beyond that, Jain is not afraid to take large bets within a single industry if he believes that the chances of all his picks falling over

at the same time for the same reason are so small as to be insignifi-
cant. Again, the Vontobel Fund - Far East Equity is cited as an example where three tobacco stocks – BAT Malaysia, ITC of India and the
delightfully named Korea Tobacco & Ginseng (KTG) add up to around
10-12% of the fund.

'The only thing they have in common is that they all make and sell
cigarettes in Asia and that they are all cash machines. The levels of
consumption in each country are different as are the legal environ-
ments, pricing and growth opportunities,' he says.

INVESTMENT STRATEGY

- Jain is a relatively flexible value investor who looks for 'growth
  businesses at discounted prices'
- Takes a long-term approach to stockpicking where the quality of
  the business is key
- Runs concentrated portfolios where potential investments are
  assessed in great detail before gaining entry
- Knowing when to sell a stock is regarded as an equally important
  discipline

Like many fund managers, Jain tries to avoid the simple, but in his
mind false, conclusions that global industry sector analysts come up
with. 'One tobacco analyst told me that she could not recommend BAT
Malaysia as a purchase because it was trading at a higher price/earn-
ings multiple than Imperial Tobacco in the UK.

'Tell me, what exactly is the connection between the two companies?
In Britain, smoking is under pressure from government health measures while in Malaysia BAT has an 80% market share, a near unregu-
lated monopoly in a country where the population is growing,' he
says. Other industries are a different matter – it would be riskier, he

says, to mix technology companies from say South Korea and Taiwan because both tend to serve the same end customer.

What is also missing from Jain's funds are Chinese companies. 'The economy there may have been growing at 10% a year but the index has lost money over the past 10 years,' he says.

Corporate governance is a big issue for Jain in China – not because he is scared of being swindled by sharp practices but simply because the level of political interference ties the hands of most companies he has looked at. 'Power consumption may have doubled but you would have lost your shirt because companies can't pass on cost increases to consumers. So the top line grows but the bottom line collapses.'

Hanging tough

Being a value investor when the markets are in bull mode can be extremely testing and Jain admits that he has had a few sleepless nights over the past year as the commodities boom largely passed his portfolio by. 'We had very little in energy or basic materials in the bull market but this is where execution gets difficult – you have to stick to your game plan,' he says.

Despite his admitted doubts, Jain is convinced that he will be proved right. 'If you believe in this concept of a 'super cycle' for commodities then you are asking for trouble. It is all opinions but the facts are scarce,' he says.

Jain searches for his justification in the annals of history. 'There have been only a couple of super cycles in the past 150 years. What happens is the price goes up, more supplies come on stream and as a producer, you have no pricing power – that is why they are called commodities.

'People say that you now have very low inventories and that's why prices will go up further but you always have low inventories at the peak of the cycle,' he says.

As an investor, Jain seeks a higher degree of conviction before putting his investors' money where his mouth is. 'The key is to ask how much do you know about a business and how much certainty you have about it on a long-term basis – the more certainty you have, the more valuable it is. If a company can grow at 3-4% a year over 20 years then that is very valuable because there are few companies which can do that.'

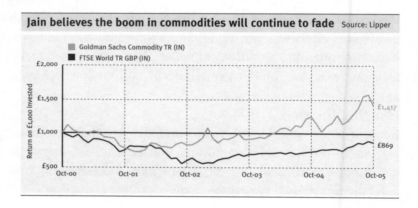

Jain believes the boom in commodities will continue to fade   Source: Lipper

Facts and knowledge run through every stage of Jain's company vetting process. He studies past annual reports and accounts to get a feel for a company and to check that what the CEO foresaw three years ago actually came about or was replaced by a different but equally vacuous vision a year later.

So Jain wants a company that delivers. He also wants one that plays fair – he prefers to avoid companies paying too little or no tax to the government that hosts their corporate headquarters. 'That might be fine today but can a company sustain that on a five-year basis – it really is too much of a risk if the government comes back to bite you,' he says.

The more Jain knows about a company, the more he can come up with an informed estimate of what he thinks it is worth and crucially whether the current market price is 25% or more below that level.

Number crunching is part of the equation, but not all of it – Jain likes to see a low price-earnings multiple adjusted for growth rate ('not perfect but still the best measure for judging long term cash flow prospects') but eschews more complex formulae.

Time not spent wading through masses of numbers is better used meeting company managements 'so I can really get a feel for what they think'. He reckons he can see far more Asian companies on road-show visits in New York than he ever could were he based in Singapore or Hong Kong, while the others are met on his frequent travels or at industry conferences.

Selling a stock – and knowing when to do it – is just as important in Jain's book. For him the art of taking profits again combines both discipline and learning from past mistakes. 'We made mistakes in the past by not applying a strict sell discipline. We just got comfortable and adjusted price targets,' he says. Today Jain trims his holdings in 5% and 10% chunks as the price target is neared.

A famous newspaper editor once said that 'comment is free but facts are sacred'. It's a saying that neatly sums up Jain's approach to investing. While the rest of the world can run around spouting about new paradigms, super cycles and (best of all) proclaiming that 'this time it's different', Jain prefers rather more certainty before dispersing his investors' money.

'It is greed and fear that drives the markets,' he says. 'People are driven more by their stomachs than their brains – that is what leaves the gap for guys like us.'

The preferred choice

Mark Lieb,

Spectrum Asset Management

by Richard Lander

The burning tarmac; drivers dicing wheel to wheel; the roar of the crowd; the smell of the oil. Oh yes, and the thrill of a fixed-interest security that makes a profit. Motor racing and fixed interest investing go together like ... well they don't really.

Unless you are Mark Lieb – ex-racing driver, vineyard owner and champion investor – in the preferred securities market. Lieb is a born and bred American who likes to succeed and be the best at everything he gets involved in. He ran with the leaders when he raced Porsches in the US Le Mans sports car series.

Today he gets his petrol kicks from his fleet of high performance sports cars that he keeps at his Long Island home (his favourite is a toss-up between two 1967 models – the lightning-fast Shelby Mustang and the all-American Chevrolet Corvette).

Having parked these monsters in the drive, Lieb can then enjoy some of the wines produced from his Lieb Cellars vines which stretch out beyond his home. The wines have had some pretty decent write-ups with the Blanc de Blanc fizz being described by the *New York*

Times wine critic Howard Goldberg as 'star-bright, refreshing, feath-er-light dry wine [with] tiny, palate-cleansing small bubbles. The wine is virtually weightless'.

Now where were we? Ah yes, the preferred securities market where Lieb has built up his Connecticut-based firm, Spectrum Asset Management, to be the dominant force.

Essentially a US phenomenon, the preferred securities market is now putting down roots in Europe. Not only are issues coming to the market priced in euros rather than dollars, but investors here are beg-ging to prick up their ears to what the market has to offer.

Having made inroads among the high net worth individuals in the private banking market, the first vehicle for retail investors was launched in October 2004 by ABN AMRO Asset Management. No sur-prise then that when the Dutch group chose to launch its Preferred Securities fund, now €115 million in size, it should turn to Lieb and Spectrum Asset Management to look after its welfare in a sub-adviso-ry capacity.

Ticking all the boxes

For those readers whose knowledge of preferred securities can best be described as minimal, do not fear – you are not alone. It is a small tributary in the great ocean that is global bond investing. Think of the many trillions of dollars that make up the US Treasury or emerging market bond markets and then size up the preferred securities mar-ket – still some way under $300 billion.

Yet just because it is small does not mean that the preferred securi-ties market deserves to be ignored. It has many qualities that make it worth a look for at least a small part of an investor's portfolio. Run through the top line of its features and you wonder why everybody doesn't invest there: high investment grade issues, yet with more than decent yields and very low default rates; plenty of liquidity; generous scope for arbitrage and mispricing; active retail interest and (uniquely for the fixed interest securities market) a listing for many of its issues on a major stock exchange.

So what lies at the core of this low risk, high-yielding market? Best described as subordinated debt, preferred securities are bonds with a few equity characteristics tagged on to them. In the pecking order of what a company owes if it should get into trouble, holders of preferred securities rank above ordinary shareholders but below bank lenders and holders of traditional senior-debt corporate bonds.

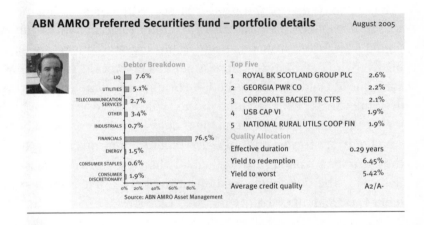

It is the equity-like features that so attract blue chip companies to raise money on the preferred securities market.

'The good news for a chief financial officer seeking to raise money is that the credit rating companies give some equity weighting which means it can help their debt/equity ratios,' explains Lieb.

They are particularly attractive for banks as they can be counted towards what is known as Tier 1 capital – the money that banks must keep aside to satisfy the financial authorities that they can be solvent whatever the circumstances and (within reason) regardless of how many nervous customers bang down the doors and demand their money back on the same day.

Not only is the preferred securities market small by fixed interest standards, it is pretty young as well. Bonds have been issued by governments, companies and assorted ne'er-do-wells for the best part of nine centuries, However, it was only in 1991 when Spain's Banco Santander became the first company to issue a preferred instrument.

After a flurry of European issuers, oil giant Texaco became the first US company to join the market in 1993, while First Bank System of the US was the first financial institution to tap the market for capital purposes in 1996.

What really makes the preferred securities market unique is the way it has opened up to the general public. Belgian dentists and their famed fetish for eurobonds aside, retail investors have tended to get involved in fixed-interest investments via mutual funds. However, someone at Goldman Sachs had the bright idea some years ago of subdividing the $1,000 face value of the typical preferred security by 40 ('Why they chose 40 I have no idea,' says Lieb) to create $25 bonds.

Not only are these bonds of a size that ordinary investors can afford, they are also traded on the floor of the New York Stock Exchange (NYSE) – 'the only place in the world where a fixed interest instrument is traded on an equity market,' Lieb says.

As a broker/dealer member of NASD (better know as the National Association of Securities Dealers and the leading private-sector regulator of the US securities industry) Lieb can have his employees down on the floor of the Big Board and trade these bonds for his clients or funds.

'It's a real leg-up for us,' he says. 'Around 99% of asset managers in the US aren't members of the NASD – it's expensive, you have to keep excess funds in the bank and file your returns every 30 days – but it really does allow for excellent execution of your orders.'

Today the preferred securities market has grown to around $255 billion, split pretty evenly between the $25 and $1,000 markets. They have some different features – for example the smaller bonds are protected from being called (or compulsorily bought back by the issuer) for five years while the $1,000 bonds get 10 years grace.

Tricks of the trade

However, both varieties are of equal rank in the pecking order of creditors should an issuing company get into trouble. Lieb has a soft spot for the $25 market.

He is a trader at heart and traders like the friction in the market that can be created when you have a real, physical market created by people rather than computers and where retail investors occasionally buy and sell with their heart rather than their head.

'You can find up to 40 basis points difference on the same issue with the same coupon between one market specialist [the NYSE's version of a market maker] and another,' he says.

CV

Born: 17 August 1950
Career: Before setting up Spectrum in 1987, Lieb was a founder, director and partner of DBL Preferred Management, a wholly owned corporate cash management subsidiary of Drexel Burnham Lambert. Prior employment included the development of the preferred stock trading desk at brokerage Mosley Hallgarten & Estabrook.

'At the same time, you also find with retail investors that they tend to pay a bit too much for Citibank and too little for an unfamiliar name such as the Swedish Export Credits Guarantee Board.

'It gives us an opportunity and is one of the reasons why we tend to be overweight in overseas preferreds. But in general it is a very liquid market and we like to have lots of names in our portfolios – between 125 to 175 names.'

The fund that Lieb runs for ABN AMRO Asset Management in

Europe has slightly different characteristics from the portfolios he manages for other clients.

'The ABN AMRO Preferred Securities fund has a short-term duration. We take a five-year portfolio and then hedge it down using Treasury futures. This takes the interest rate risk out of the portfolio and makes it very suitable for very risk averse investors,' he says.

A widening spectrum

Lieb's Spectrum operation started up in 1987 and is now by far the biggest player in the preferred securities market, with around $13.5 billion under management. His car racing days aside, he has an intriguing background, having spent much of the 1980s at Drexel Burnham Lambert running their preferred stock department.

That was of course the time that Michael Milken was making a very public name for himself in junk bonds, running operations in such a

---

Not a lot of people know that:

Lieb studied meteorology at the Kent State University in Ohio for two years. He still reads and studies the weather closely.

---

way that led to both his and Drexel's demise. 'I didn't know him well and there were things going on there that I didn't know about,' he says. 'But it was a very good time for me there and I learned a lot.'

Spectrum was set up after Lieb left Drexel and decided against joining another Wall Street name. By leaping on the nascent preferred securities market he has become what he calls 'a big fish in a small pond', a situation he clearly enjoys.

He still runs his business from Hartford in Connecticut and remains

independent of Principal Global Investors, the Iowa based money
manager which bought his firm in 2001.

Principal is a huge operation and runs around 10 times as much
money as Spectrum does in property, fixed income and equities. The
tie-up has been good for both companies – Principal's market reach
has helped Spectrum grow its assets from just $1 billion at the time of
its purchase.

The tie-up with Principal has also given him access to its ranks of
credit analysts to supplement the three he has in head office. While
default rates in preferred securities are so low as to be minimal, Lieb
is not complacent. 'We spend an inordinate time dealing with credit,'
he says.

If a company does default on its preferred securities, it will probably
have made the headlines for burning through its bank lines of credit,
its equity commitments and then its senior debt.

The financial disasters of WorldCom and Enron are examples of
companies whose preferred issues are now only good for papering the
cloakroom walls.

Lieb's portfolios had neither. 'The risk of course is that preferred
securities rank as junior to normal senior debt if a company gets into
trouble so that the recovery rate is lower,' he says.

But as he points out with default rates so low, the yield margin over
corporate senior debt (around 100 basis points) and US Treasury bonds
(up to 175 basis points) seems a fairly generous one. That margin also
goes some way to compensating investors for having their bonds called
– an event happening with increasing frequency now as companies refinance debt issued when interest rates were much higher.

However, with new issues coming to the market all the time,
nobody is likely to run out of material to buy any time soon.
'Issuance is pretty steady and we have a good calendar so that I think
the market should be able to move above the $300 billion level quite
soon,' says Lieb.

Golden rules

Knowing which issues to go for in the primary and secondary market is what Lieb believes is the key to getting this market right. 'Credit is first and foremost,' he says.

Rule number one is simple – avoid any companies on the shopping list of leveraged buyout companies that seek to take them over with a mountain of high-yielding paper. If the takeover happens, any investment grade bonds immediately take on junk status.

Rule number two is to keep a close eye on the business conditions of the industry that issuers come from. The biggest blowouts in 2005 – in all the credit markets and not just preferred securities – came from the US car sector where manufacturers battled on the one hand with reluctant consumers and on the other with growing burdens for employee healthcare and pension costs. The results were not pretty but Lieb says his portfolios escaped the worst.

Car crashes

'We owned Ford, General Motors and Daimler Chrysler and altogether we had around 3% of our portfolios in the car industry,' he says. 'However, about a year ago we didn't like the look of the way things were going. Car sales were moving ahead strongly but the incentives the manufacturers were offering to get people to come in to the showrooms and buy them were too great.

'So we scaled down our holdings in a big way to the point where they now account for around 0.25% of what we own in total. After that, the ratings agencies jumped all over them and relegated their bond issues to junk status,' he says.

Part of the game is to second guess the credit rating agencies because it is their actions, rather than the underlying health of the companies, that may be a more important factor in determining what happens to bond prices. 'These car companies are not going out of business. General Motors and Ford must have at least $75 billion of cash between them and around $10 billion of debt obligations.

'But the agencies have been burned in the past by not downgrading quickly enough and have become very skittish, so I think that it is very likely that they will do more downgrades now than they have in the past. We do use them but for the most part we prefer to rely on our own wits.'

Exporting expertise

Those wits have been strengthened in recent years by substantial expenditure on information technology at Spectrum's back office. Having handled individual mandates for corporate treasurers, pension funds and endowment bodies for the first decade of its existence, Spectrum went in to the sub-advisory business in 1997 to farm out its expertise to other asset management houses.

Nomura launched the first preferred securities open-ended fund in Japan, part of an international expansion which led to the launch of the ABN AMRO Preferred Securities fund in 2004.

Lieb's big break on this side of the business came through a mandate to launch a series of closed-end funds (akin to investment trusts) for Nuveen Investments, a Chicago-based money manager whose principal expertise was in municipal bonds.

'The Nuveen funds raised $5 billion in 16 months,' says Lieb. 'We spent $500,000 upgrading the back office and carried out 28,000 trades for those funds and delivered every one of them without a mistake.'

A sense of proportion

You might look at the key points of preferred securities and ask why a fixed-income investor would want to put his or her money anywhere else. To recap, the upside outweighs the downside by a big margin – a great yield on investment grade paper, low default rates, a liquid market and the chance to make an extra few points here and there because there are so many retail investors in the market.

It is a good question, admits Lieb, but despite being the preferred securities evangelist he is, he is not about to suggest that you deposit all your eggs in his basket. 'It is a tool in fixed income – not the be all and end all of the market – and should play a small part in any allocation you have there. I just don't believe people should see this end of the market as the holy grail and say 'I'll sell all my senior debt,' he says.

Pressed for a number he suggests that perhaps 5-10% of a fixed income portfolio should be in preferred, perhaps something a little higher for individuals who can't get such easy access to the more conventional senior bond market with its face values of $1,000.

What really does upset Lieb is when institutional investors snub preferred securities on the advice of their consultants who say they

---

INVESTMENT STRATEGY

- Lieb believes the key to success in the preferred securities is knowing how to spot potential losers
- Tries to second guess the credit ratings agencies as their actions, rather than the underlying health of the company are often bigger influence of bond prices
- Keeps a close eye on business climate of the industry that issuers come from

---

are all a bit complex and – having some characteristics of both equities and bonds – fall into the apparently unpardonable sin of being neither fish nor fowl.

'Most consultants are not really forward thinking enough to understand an asset class that can look like a square peg in a round hole,' he says. 'On top of that they are not prepared to understand how it works. It really is pretty simple but some of them will say no and come up with 16 reasons to justify their advice.' One gets the impression that not too many consultants make it onto the Spectrum Christmas card list. Nonetheless when people get to know how preferred securities work they tend to take to them in a big way. 'Insurance companies in the US love them because they find that the market is the best place to get a high investment grade yield, while corporate treasurers like them as a place to hold their cash for the short term in a liquid market,' he says. 'Now we are making inroads into the private banking and the high net worth individual markets in Europe.'

For a man who likes to be the fastest and the best in what he does, Lieb has no particular desire to be the biggest player in fixed-interest securities. He is not an asset gatherer for the sake of it and sees Spectrum going from its present $16 billion capacity to perhaps $18 billion before growth tapers. It must be time to break out the wine.

The inside edge

Jan Luthman and Stephen Bailey

Walker Crips Weddle Beck

by Richard Lander

Many years ago the legendary sports promoter Mark McCormack wrote a business advice book entitled: *What they don't teach you at Harvard Business School.*

The gist of the book was that those who got out there and got their hands dirty would learn far more about running a business than those who spent the best part of two years and £50,000 working through endless case studies in a classroom.

If Jan Luthman were to write a similar book about how to be a fund manager, it would probably be called something like: *Don't just invest in a company – go out and run one.* Luthman spent many years in Africa and the Middle East doing just that – building up and running businesses – and is convinced that the experience of working on some of the corporate world's wilder frontiers has given him a significant advantage when it comes to investing in them.

Not that the two men are similar. McCormack, who died in 2003, was one of the sports world's great showmen who operated from his luxury home in Florida. Luthman, along with co-manager Stephen Bailey, runs two UK equity funds for Walker Crips Weddle Beck, a small broking and asset management house situated on the less glamorous edge of the City of London.

Low key the operation may be (the CF Walker Crips UK Growth fund and CF Walker Crips Equity Income fund have just over £120 million assets between them) but the funds and their managers are consistently first-quartile performers. More often than not they make the top-five performance lists, and have created a small but significant and loyal fan base of investors.

In the know
And one of the reasons for this success, Luthman maintains, is the 18 years he spent in the field before taking up formal fund management at the ripe age of 56.

'Managing a range of businesses in a variety of locations gives an understanding of companies that matters,' he says. 'It is not the be all and end all of investing, but it gives a real advantage at the edge.'

If you have been there, done that and bought (or indeed made, marketed, packaged and sold) the T-shirt, reading a dull-as-dishwater company report and accounts suddenly takes on real vibrancy and colour, he says.

'If you have tried to develop or turn around a small company then you understand the numbers in a way that those who haven't been there can't,' he says. 'The story behind the numbers leaps off the page – storm warning cones like slowing stock turn, thinning margins, extending debtors, stretching creditors – you can really feel the guy sweating.'

And it is not just the interpretation of the numbers that puts Luthman and Bailey one step ahead. There is what might loosely be called the Dilbert Factor – interpreting the nuances of office politics, and what companies mean as opposed to what they say.

'If you've been there yourself, you understand in a very personal way why managers don't always make the choice best suited to shareholders. They don't want to have to make the big write-down on their watch,' he says.

A distinguished line-up united by talent ...

Chris Burvill (p15-25)
Gartmore

Chris Burvill has excelled at value-based equity income investing for 18 years. His talent for evaluating stocks is underpinned by clear ideas about the sort of business he wants to invest in and he meets at least 200 companies every year.

Alex Darwall (p27-37)
Jupiter Asset Management

Alex Darwall has a knack for backing some of Europe's most dynamic companies. The EU may often be cursed for its backward economic policies but Darwall looks for businesses that transcend political obstacles and many of his favoured stocks have a global outlook.

Rajiv Jain (p39-49)
Vontobel Asset Management Inc.

The value investment process that Rajiv Jain and his team have built is centred on quality rather than finding a collection of beaten-up stocks that the market has overlooked. This discipline, combined with the skill to recognise when to sell a holding, has given Jain a consistent edge.

Mark Lieb (p51-61)
Spectrum Asset Management

Mark Lieb invests in preferred securities, which are basically bonds with a few equity characteristics tagged on to them. Essentially a US phenomenon, the preferred securities market is now putting down roots in Europe and there aren't many better than Lieb to spread the word.

Jan Luthman and Stephen Bailey (p63-75)
Walker Crips Weddle Beck

Jan Luthman and Stephen Bailey have an uncanny grasp of the 'big picture' and its potential impact on the stockmarket. Much of their time is spent identifying top-down themes to build a portfolio that is in harmony with national and international economic, political and social influences.

David Mitchinson (p77-87)
JPMorgan Asset Management

Jens Moestrup Rasmussen (p101-111)
Sparinvest Fondsmaeglerselskab

At just 28 David Mitchinson has rapidly made a name for himself as one of the best Japan fund managers in the business. A keen eye for companies that are embracing the economic and financial reforms of the 'New Japan' continues to push Mitchinson ahead of the pack.

Jens Moestrup Rasmussen is in many ways a classic value investor who prefers to buy stocks that he believes are intrinsically worth 100% more than their market value. However, he has a touch of the fixed interest fund manager and assesses a company's downside before anything else.

Jonathan Platt and Sajiv Vaid (p89-99)
Royal London Asset Management

Jonathan Platt and Sajiv Vaid stay one step ahead of their rivals by exploiting misunderstood areas of the bond market. With ever more varieties of debt being issued opportunities abound for fund managers such as Platt and Vaid who have the experience and skill to look far beyond the analysis produced by credit ratings agencies.

Ted Scott (p113-123)
F&C Asset Management

Andrew Sutherland (p125-135)
Standard Life Investments

Ted Scott has made his name running ethical investment funds but his knowledge of the wider stockmarket is a key contributor to his impressive track record. Just because a stock is valued attractively compared with the universe of his ethical companies does not make it an immediate buy if it is wildly overvalued within the market as a whole.

Andrew Sutherland has spent more than 20 years in the investment industry but he is far from complacent. As anomalies become increasingly hard to find, Sutherland is pushing his fixed-interest team to open up new frontiers to stay a step ahead of the competition.

Dissembling becomes ingrained up and down the corporate food chain. 'If a salesman foresees sales doubling in the next year, he'll forecast 25% so as to provide himself with a safety net and maximise bonus potential. Similarly, the sales manager will forecast a 20% increase, and the sales director will incorporate a 10% uplift in his report to the board.

'On the other hand, if the salesman (and his chain of command) thinks his market will collapse, he'll never admit it. Instead he'll dream up a superficially credible forecast, and hope like hell something comes along to save him. If it doesn't, at least he'll have kept his job for a year,' he says.

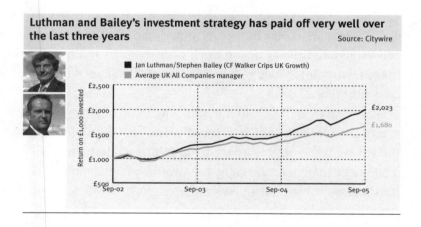

Luthman and Bailey's investment strategy has paid off very well over the last three years

Source: Citywire

- Jan Luthman/Stephen Bailey (CF Walker Crips UK Growth)
- Average UK All Companies manager

This is one reason, he says, why analysts chronically underestimate both the upturns and downturns of the corporate cycle. 'They just don't understand corporate life and politics.'

'And,' he adds, 'beware the chief executive who leads his company into new and uncharted territories. Talk of developing new value-adding technologies, new exciting markets, new high margin products can be very beguiling, but ask yourself: Do existing staff have the appropriate skills, and the board the necessary understanding?'

He is particularly wary of companies that wander around the globe to plant their expansionist flags, expecting things to be as they are back home.

Having worked in what he calls 'some of the more exciting areas of the world' he notes euphemistically that 'notions of corporate governance vary greatly from place to place'. The hairs on the back of his neck prickle when he sees UK companies commit large chunks of shareholders' money to ventures in uncharted territories. This can involve doing business in a country where one can neither read, write or speak the language and where local management will be reporting to a UK board bereft of experience, knowledge or understanding. It could also be a place where what might diplomatically be termed the 'business etiquette' appropriate to the region sits uneasily with western notions of corporate governance and cannot always be easily accommodated in the framework of a western multinational. All of these factors introduce risk, but is that risk reflected in the valuation, asks Luthman?

There is a right way and a wrong way to do business overseas. 'The international landscape is littered with the debris of those who took the wrong route, and it would be unfair to quote names,' he says 'but a modest example of the right way would be households goods maker PZ Cussons, which has been trading in West Africa for more than 100 years.

'I worked in West Africa for many years and knew them well. More than a century of experience, contacts and know-how mean that they understand how to do business in those parts of the world; have a realistic awareness and understanding of the risks; know the qualities that make for effective management; and that local management are reporting to a board that understands the environment in which they are operating.'

PZ Cussons was chosen by Luthman and Bailey for a particular reason – they wanted a company that could take advantage of the rising level of personal incomes in developing oil exporting countries.

Dynamic forces

And it is themes – the big political, economic and social drivers shaping and reshaping the world around us – that lie behind the way Luthman and Bailey put together their investment portfolios. They start with the big issues and follow them down to see how they play out in terms of winners and losers at the company level.

CV: Jan Luthman

Born: 1 April 1945

Career: Following his graduation as a Civil Engineer in 1967 Luthman undertook a range of international appointments and managed a variety of heavy equipment and oilfield dealerships in the Middle East and Africa. An active private investor, he was among the first to pass the Securities Association exams in Investment Analysis and Fund Management upon his return to the UK. He joined Hambros Bank as an institutional sales manager in 1988, moving on to Perpetual four years later, where he became senior investment writer. However, his fund management skills lay largely untapped until he joined Walker Crips in 2000. Now, working alongside colleague Stephen Bailey, he runs the CF Walker Crips UK Growth and Equity Income funds, and the new Collins Stewart UK Growth fund.

Luthman reckons today's macro-economic themes and issues are both powerful and unprecedented. 'We have themes such as global warming, ageing populations, the internet, telecommunications and globalisation, none of which have been around before,' he says. 'You have to structure a portfolio so that it is in harmony with the issues that are arising at both national and international levels.'

And that is why, for example, Luthman has a big position in UK life assurance companies, seen by many other fund managers as dead in the water, poisoned chalices or a combination of the two. Luthman instead sees them as investment opportunities.

'There is a growing need for people to save for their old age and an improving political and regulatory environment. Meanwhile, employment is growing among the generation most inclined to save and the savings ratio has started to rise again,' he says. 'In addition, the life assurance industry enjoys earnings and margins resilience that would be the envy of much of the British economy. Take, for example, British industry's number one worry – competition from low-cost regions of the world. The life industry has regulatory immunity to that. Then take another major concern of British manufacturers – the squeeze on margins from rising costs for energy and raw materials. The life industry doesn't burn oil or bash metal.

'Then consider that, if shoppers stop shopping, shops go bust pretty quickly. But if savers stop saving, life companies have huge funds under management that will carry on generating management fees for many years to come. This means great resilience of earnings, plus embedded cash flows that could make life companies prime targets for acquisitions if their valuations dropped further. In other words, they offer a combination of earnings growth, earnings and margin resilience, and possible acquisition upside that current valuations don't seem to recognise,' he says.

Prelude to a bull market
Talking of takeovers, Luthman is particularly pleased that, while most other strategists saw only gloom and doom at the back end of 2004, he forecast that the UK stockmarket was positioned rather nicely for a continued bull run and an upsurge in corporate activity, as indeed came to pass.

'The wellspring for today's acquisition-driven bull market was globalisation. It brought with it concerns that investment and employment would migrate from high-cost regions to low-cost regions. In response, central banks of industrialised economies adopted "accommodative" monetary policies in an attempt to stimulate demand and employment that would otherwise not have been there, and allow industrialised economies some breathing space in which to restructure.

Investors tended to focus on the capacity for globalisation, and global competition, to depress earnings. However, what they failed to foresee was that a combination of ample money supply, very low interest rates and modest valuations were providing the ingredients that would whet the appetites of venture capitalists and corporate predators. To this appetising mix was added the spice of IFRS (International Financial Reporting Standards), which, by removing the requirement for annual goodwill depreciation, transformed the earnings enhanc-

---

Not a lot of people know that:

Investors are not the only benefactors of Luthman's creative powers. He runs a website of children's stories (www.fables.co.uk) where visitors are free to dip in to the latest adventures of Jonathan the Fastest Snail in The Meadow and other characters.

---

ing capabilities of acquisitions. The ingredients were in place for a feeding frenzy, and those saw the signs have prospered.

'We had already seen asset price bubbles build in housing, bonds and commodities. Without higher interest rates to suck up the liquidity that had built up in these asset classes, it seemed not unreasonable to expect that it would flow on into equity markets,' he says.

Luthman is particularly adept at reading the runes of official economic statistics. Again, he can apparently see more within the dry numbers they contain than the average fund manager or strategist.

One thing that has struck him during 2005 has been the contrast between the substantial increase in corporation tax receipts, and the very modest rise in VAT receipts. This implies, he argues, that UK plc is not producing much more than it did last year, but is making a great deal more money doing so.

'What we are seeing,' suggests Luthman, 'is earnings improvement, rather than earnings growth, and the two have very different implications for our investment strategy going forward. Acquisitions are driving restructuring, and shareholders are benefiting, but employees are beginning to feel the strain as wage growth slows and unemployment rises.'

Globalisation, he argues, and the monetisation that it triggered, has created an environment in which 'it is becoming easier to make money but harder to earn a living'.

Warning signs

The evidence of the latter is all around: wage growth in the private sector is slowing, unemployment claimant count has increased every month since January, distressed debtors are petitioning for their own bankruptcy in unprecedented numbers, and home repossessions are rising rapidly.

This will be one of the themes as Luthman and Bailey seek to position their portfolio for how they see the world and the UK developing over the next decade.

'Wage growth may be slowing,' says Luthman, 'but wages and benefits are still at levels unsustainable in a globalised economy, and the process has much further to go. Directives on wages and benefits that ignore the realities of competition – whether from immigrants or across the world – will ensure that Britain's army of 259,000 unemployed young citizens expands and ages, imposing a growing burden on the economy and society to which they belong, but from which they are increasingly being excluded. Consumer spending is trending downwards, and retailers who would clutch at the straw of jobs growth should note that the greatest growth has been amongst those least inclined to spend – men and women past retirement age. Meanwhile, those most disposed to profligacy have suffered the greatest loss of jobs. Over the year to September 2005, the number of 18-24 year-olds claiming benefits rose 11.2%. Women in that age group claiming long-term benefits rose a staggering 33%. In such an environment it is difficult to view valuations within much of the leisure and pleasure industry as anything other than optimistic,' says Luthman.

Resourceful strategies

A major theme in Luthman and Bailey's thinking at present, and which provides a backdrop to their portfolio, is the resources sector,

---

CV: Stephen Bailey

Born: 13 May 1967
Career: Bailey began his career in money management in 1985 as a with stockbrokers Statham, Duff, Stoop and followed this with a year at Sheppards & Chase, before joining Walker Crips Weddle Beck in 1987. He was promoted to investment manager in the early 1990s, then appointed to the board as investment director in the late 1990s. His responsibilities include co-managing the Walker Crips UK Growth and UK Equity Income funds, and the new Collins Stewart offshore UK Growth fund alongside colleague Jan Luthman.

---

in particular the determination of major and growing powers to secure supplies of energy and raw materials. 'Just look at the intense political manoeuvring in the oil and gas-rich regions around the Caspian Sea by China, Russia, India and the US, all of it further complicated by the presence and involvement of Iran,' he says. Reaching into the history books, Luthman sees today's quest for resource supremacy as being 'a bit like the land grab in Africa by major European powers 100 years ago'.

Luthman and Bailey do not see these geo-political drivers as likely to wane, and if this global dynamic is going to remain in force, 'we have to ask ourselves how should we structure our portfolio?' says Luthman.

The response has been to build a portfolio within a framework that is prepared to invest in those who own resources, but seeks to avoid those dependent upon them. It is a portfolio that has a substantial bias towards what might be termed the 'de-materialised' economy – industries such as life assurance, specialist financials and telecommunications.

Not a lot of people know that:

Bailey's interest in the financial world extends beyond the rigours of fund management and he is a keen stockmarket historian. To offset the intense, disciplined mental activity he plays hard too and enjoys cricket, rugby and golf.

Luthman and Bailey's move into telecoms is relatively recent, reflecting what they see as fundamental changes in the industry. They avoided the sector in 2003 and 2004 – 'excess capacity, the risks of technological obsolescence, and a regulatory regime that limited profits but didn't limit losses made a poor investment case' – but now the rapid growth in non-voice data traffic, and the diminishing influence of regulators in an increasingly global industry offer the prospect of pricing power and earnings growth.

Picking the themes is one skill – choosing the right companies to benefit from such drivers is quite another. Here Luthman and Bailey look at what they term 'the validity of the business model' – its capacity to capture the benefits of a theme, or provide protection from the downside. 'Financial strength is particularly important at a time of global excess capacity,' he says. 'It provides the strength to develop new and better products, to market more aggressively, to acquire weaker competitors, or simply to outlast them. It offers great strategic power.'

Although Luthman enjoys digging and delving in the remoter corners of statistical tables such as those churned out by the Office of National Statistics, neither he nor Bailey see this process as offering significant opportunity to add value at company level. 'You're unlikely to discover a nugget of gold if all you do is crunch and sieve numbers that have already been crunched and sieved by a hundred others,' he says.

'What we're looking for are the unquantifiable influences: the political, social and economic themes that affect the way we live and conduct business, themes that emerge, evolve, mutate and interact, and which eventually feed through into market valuations. In short, the issues for which it is difficult, if not impossible, to develop analytical software, and which for that very reason offer opportunities to identify hidden value.'

Incoming challenges

It is doubtful that any software program could analyse the world and the way it is changing with such perception as Luthman does. He reckons that the way we live and work is being, and will continue to be, radically reshaped by the forces of globalisation.

'There are some parallels with the Industrial Revolution two centuries ago. Ultimately, the transformation from agricultural to industrial economy created a wealthier nation, and brought greatly improved standards of living. The snag was that ultimately took several decades to arrive, during which time the process of change brought extended periods of great social suffering. Today, we may well be about to enter a similar period. Globalisation and the shift from an industrial to a knowledge-based economy may well eventually create a wealthier and healthier global economy, but "eventually" could take many years to arrive.

'We do not know, any more than our Victorian forebears did, what future enterprises will replace the familiar industries of today. Until they do, though, growing numbers of our community employed may find themselves stripped of the ability to earn a living, as capital and

---

INVESTMENT STRATEGY

- Spend much time identifying top-down themes and strive to build a portfolio that is in harmony with national and international economic, political and social influences
- Refine shortlist on basis of factors including, validity of business model in light of macro issues, management credibility, financial strength, relative valuation
- Conduct ongoing trawls for valuation anomalies, correlation break downs, shifts in commercial strategy, shifts in nature of business, hidden signals in financial, trading and strategy statements

---

employment migrate to regions where lower costs provide competitive advantage. How we as a society handle this issue will be a substantial challenge,' he says.

Luthman is aware of his reputation for sounding like the harbinger of doom – indeed, his office desk bears a gift from his wife of *Eeyore's Little Book of Gloom*. But he maintains that he is decidedly not a pessimist, more a realist with an acute ability to analyse what is happening to the world that we live in. Indeed, he looks forward with considerable optimism. 'Entrepreneurial capitalism has been alive for millennia and has served us very well. It is not about to roll over and die,' he says. 'On the contrary it is thriving. History has shown us time and time again that periods of great change bring with them great opportunities, and today is no different. Investors with vision, who position themselves appropriately, will prosper.'

It was the philosopher George Santayana who said: 'Those who cannot remember the mistakes of history are condemned to repeat them.' You can ignore what Luthman says, or disagree with him – but look back 20 years and see what has emerged since then, from satellite television to ipods, email to blogs and from worries about our pensions to concern about the environment. Look too, at how the industrial giants of then are faring today, and which of today's most successful companies even existed. He might just have a point.

Our man in Japan

David Mitchinson,

JPMorgan Asset Management

by Richard Lander

We live in an age of undue caution where people in the investment industry speak with forked tongues – and then only after consultation with their spin doctors – for fear of offending the regulators, litigious investors, the environmental lobby and, who knows, the Save The Whales campaign and the Canine Defence League.

So it is rather refreshing when someone comes straight out and says: 'I believe index X will be at Y by 2008 and here are the reasons. Yes, I know there are no guarantees of anything in this world but I am paid to make these forecasts and this is my best guess.'

Step forward then, David Mitchinson, manager of the £390 million JPM Japan fund, who is firmly of the belief (and has been for some time) that the Tokyo market's Nikkei 225 index, currently around 14,700, will pass through the 20,000 barrier within two to three years.

'That prediction is not crazy or wild, although it was a little bolder when I first said it' says Mitchinson. 'But it amounts to a rise of around 35% over two years which is not completely aggressive.'

Indeed it is not, especially when compared to other forecasters who have put a number on an index. For example, US soothsayers James Glassman and Kevin Hassett chose September 1999 to publish *Dow 36,000: The New Strategy for Profiting from the Coming Rise in the*

Stock Market. That most venerable of stockmarket measures then stood at 11,200. It peaked just shy of 12,000 in January 2000 and has not approached that level since. Plenty of copies of the book are now being sold on Amazon for 10p should you be interested.

This time it really is different

Mitchinson is made of far stronger stuff and so too, he believes is the Japanese market. 'There is really good upside here – some stocks are still mispriced by up to 100% – and by making this prediction I want to help people concentrate on the fact that something really different from before is happening,' he said.

'People say "we are underweight Japan and should we go neutral?" We're saying, yes, definitely go overweight. People are concerned that they have missed the boat and should wait for a big pull back, but we think this is different.'

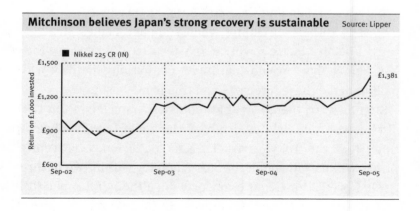

Life has certainly been different over the last 12 months for Mitchinson. Not only did he move to JPMorgan Asset Management from Framlington, where he had blazed ahead of almost all his rivals by nearly doubling his investors' money in under 30 months (the peer average rise was 7%) but he also moved his working base from London to Tokyo. The two changes were intimately connected.

'At Framlington I had colleagues I really respected but none of them apart from me seriously followed the Japanese market so they could only talk in general parallels,' he says. 'Here I can discuss stocks in depth with the team here and you can see what is happening on the ground, even just by going on the tube and looking at what is happening around you.'

Two huge questions were asked about Mitchinson when he made the move. First – how would he fare in what was perceived to be the rather more *dirigiste* atmosphere of a giant house like JPMorgan after his first job in the much smaller and avowedly manager-centric atmosphere of Framlington?

Mitchinson says this has not been an issue. He is just as unconstrained by index weightings as he was back in London and if he dislikes a stock, then it does not go in the portfolio no matter what it says in the index tables.

The second question (especially from the more elderly and cynical members of the investment world) was whether this young whippersnapper, still just 28, was as good as he was cracked up to be or whether he had just enjoyed a massive dose of beginner's luck? The numbers speak for themselves – after taking over in October 2004 and spending two months culling an underperforming portfolio, Mitchinson's fund has outpaced its benchmark and its peers in 2005.

Positive signs

If there is any one company that sums up why Mitchinson is so enthusiastic about Japan, it is financial services group Nikko Cordial where its Nikko Asset Management arm is being transformed by Bill Wilder, one of the Tokyo market's most renowned figures who joined last year from Fidelity.

'Nikko Asset Management has huge assets but they're mostly in the money market,' he says. 'Wilder has come in, got rid of a lot of people and is incentivising the others to get people into real funds. With some very basic changes you could see fees rising from 2 to 50 basis points.'

Like many of Mitchinson's stock choices, Nikko Cordial is both poorly researched by analysts and plays to the zeitgeist of what you might call the New Japan. The crushing general election victory of Junichiro Koizumi in the autumn of 2005, which focused on the liberalisation and reform of the Post Office, was crucial in this respect.

As the world's biggest savings bank, the Post Office holds the savings of millions of Japanese who tucked their money away during the traumatic decade-long period of deflation.

'Now that money is rolling over and paying far less interest. People like ourselves, Nikko Cordial and others are all beginning to target retail investors who are feeling a bit more confident about finding better returns for their money,' he says.

Nobody is expecting Japan's army of savers to leap instantly into high-risk equities but Mitchinson sees a gradual move into assets such as direct and collective real estate, fixed interest stocks and foreign bonds 'all of which will provide better fees for those who manage them'.

Building stronger foundations

In fact Mitchinson sees what is happening as a replay of the 1980s and 1990s in the US and Britain as asset managers started to help people invest their new-found wealth more strategically into investment funds and introduce the concept of long-term wealth management.

The return of confidence to the property market is crucial as its collapse in the 1990s was central to the economic trauma that overwhelmed the entire Japanese economy. If you think the UK market looks a little toppy and might be heading for a gentle decline, recall that the bursting of the Japanese property bubble saw Tokyo land values collapse by about 75% over 15 years after doubling in the late 1980s.

So stable property prices, as Tokyo now has, are very significant. 'I just saw a house-building company and they are reporting more people coming into the showroom,' Mitchinson says. 'That is not yet feeding through into sales but you don't go to a showroom just for fun. When people start buying that will lead to a pick-up in other areas such as construction, furniture, bathroom suites and the economy as a whole.'

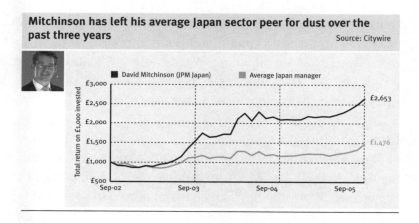

Mitchinson has left his average Japan sector peer for dust over the past three years

Source: Citywire

Company matters

While paying close attention to the sectors that appear to be the most likely to benefit as Japan wakes up from its lost decade, the driving force behind Mitchinson's investment process, and one which he shares with the rest of the JPMorgan team, is to focus on the quality of each company to see whether it is worthy to be included in his small and select portfolio, which holds around 50 stocks on average.

'With my Framlington background I am instinctively drawn to looking more to individual stocks rather than the sectors they come from,' Mitchinson says. 'The ethos of my investment process is to buy good companies at the wrong prices and watch them grow for three to four years. Sometimes they do nothing and that can be very frustrating but then there are always the ones that do grow.'

The quality of management in Japan is even more crucial than in other markets. Economic events slow down and speed up elsewhere but it is essentially business as usual. By contrast, the change from deflation to inflation in Japan is one of seismic proportions that requires a company's management to cope with a completely new set of skills.

'A new strategy is needed and that is polarising the good companies from the bad ones, with the good ones concentrating on matters such as return on invested capital and taking decisive steps so that they can reward us as shareholders. We are, after all, lending our capital to people so that they can grow their business and we would much rather give it to people who will take care of it for us,' he says.

Close encounters

Making a true assessment of a company's management means meeting them in their droves. On an average day Mitchinson will have one or two meetings although he recently managed to squeeze in sessions with a carbon fibre maker, a business hotel chain, a housing business and an office furniture group all on the same day. His colleagues meet other businesses as well and as a firm, the Japan office of JPMorgan Asset Management gets to contact every company on its core coverage list each quarter.

'We do this even if we think the company is boring. You have to keep forcing yourself to evaluate every company and ask yourself "is it getting any better?" The answer might be "No it is still awful" but it could also be "No, it really is not as bad as I thought it was and there just might be something quite interesting here." The aim is to fully understand the business model and strategy of every company we invest in.'

This intense system of scrutiny is one that other investment professionals in the Tokyo market are now beginning to latch on to. 'There probably are more fund managers here doing this now than there were two or three years ago,' he says. 'But we probably place more emphasis on this than others. The whole process is designed simply to find good companies and good businesses and get the right stocks into the portfolio.'

A case in Point

One stock that is a real favourite of Mitchinson on account of the quality of its management is Point Inc, a fashion retailer which accounts for 2.4% of his portfolio and is his 10th largest holding.

What impresses Mitchinson so much is the way that Point's management has expanded from its original single brand, Lowry's Farm, into a host of others including Global Work.

INVESTMENT STRATEGY

- Focuses more on individual companies than sectors and aims to buy good business that have been mis-priced
- Hunts among under-researched stocks with a keen eye for those with dynamic managements that are embracing the economic and financial reforms of the 'New Japan'
- Meets with at least one or two companies every day

Just as Gap split its market in the US by developing the value Old Navy Brand and the upmarket Banana Republic label, so Point is slicing and dicing in Japan. Lowry's Farm targets twentysomething women wanting 'trendy items at reasonable prices in proper styles' according to the Point website while Global Work 'offers casual fashion for the baby-boomer generation and their children'.

Mitchinson likes the strategy. 'Point has gone for new segments in the market and is one of Japan's leading specialty retailers. They get lots of efficiencies by making single daily deliveries to shops located in the same shopping mall,' he says. The shares have soared but with rapid growth on the cards, earnings should rise at around 35% a year for the next four or five years – double the stock's current price/earnings ratio.

'At some point the stock could be seen as being too expensive for us to hold but the management of Point continues to surprise everyone concerned,' he says. 'They have done all of this against the background of a weak economy, so when the economy picks up it should do even better. It all comes down to company management selling the right product and using the right techniques.'

Mitchinson has a tendency to major on small and medium cap stocks because with low coverage by stockbroking analysts, that is where he is most likely to find pricing inefficiencies. And even when analysts do shine a light on the companies that he likes to target, he believes they are aiming it in the wrong place.

'Sometimes fund managers are better placed than analysts to see things,' he says. 'We find many sell-side analysts myopic and they don't always stand back and look at the bigger picture.'

Giant battles

However, large caps do feature in Mitchinson's portfolio, especially those from the financial sector and he sees the same split between good and bad management in the larger end of the scale.

For example, in consumer electronics he contrasts Matsushita and its success in LCD and plasma television sets with Sony. While Sony was the company that invented the world's first portable music player decades ago in the shape of the Walkman, it has totally and utterly conceded the battle for MP3 digital music players to Apple, which has walked off with Sony's credentials for brilliant product design.

At the heart of Sony's problems in MP3 players was faction-driven internal politics. While Sony's recorded music division was horrified at the thought of devices that could easily copy songs from computers, the consumer product division knew people would not buy anything that made copying difficult. The music division won and Sony lags ever further behind Apple.

CV

Born: 4 December 1976
Career: Mitchinson spent six years at Framlington before he joined JPMorgan Asset Management in the summer of 2004. He was initially an Asian equity analyst at Framlington before he took charge of the Framlington Japan fund with considerable success. His responsibilities also included the Japan elements of International Growth, EAFE, and pension and sector funds (Financial and Technology). The move to JPMorgan also meant a move to Japan for Mitchinson who now works out of the group's Tokyo office at the helm of the JPM Japan fund.

Matsushita on the other hand saw a new world emerging and learned to cope with changing conditions. 'They restructured and made some tough decisions which Sony avoided by ignoring the difficult questions. You can't do that these days,' Mitchinson says. The market, as it tends to do, has rewarded those who make the right decisions. Shares in Sony have risen around 6% in 2005 while those in Matsushita are up by about half and stand at a 52-week high.

As ever, technology is an important component of the Japanese market and one that demands special attention because of its very high capital demands and the ongoing battle to sustain and generate profits. Mitchinson likes the gearing effect of, for example, microchip makers who lock into a market such as flat-panel television sets where demand takes off exponentially in the shops as prices drop below certain key levels.

But the pendulum can swing both ways and it is just as easy to over-estimate a company's fortunes when a product cycle goes against them. 'If sales are low, margins fall and that leads to excess inventory. That in turns forces you to discount and then innovate more,' he says. 'In the end you find that a company is running fast simply to stand still.'

Mitchinson himself likes to run pretty fast at work. Apart from the UK retail fund he also looks after a couple of Japanese smaller companies vehicles – a UK onshore investment trust and an offshore Sicav fund. Like his retail fund 'they have not had the performance that people deserve in the past' and Mitchinson says that it is his aim to put things right.

Not a lot of people know that:

Mitchinson's deft touch extends beyond stockpicking – he is a keen tennis player and is a black belt in that most ancient of Japanese arts, origami.

However, he has no desire at all to extend his repertoire to encompass a Japanese hedge fund. 'Everybody is completely obsessed with hedge funds but I prefer to spend time looking at the best names rather than searching for stocks to short at the beginning of a bull market.'

The place to be

Mitchinson's enthusiasm for the Japanese stockmarket is evident. 'It is very exciting to be working in a market that has such confidence. The Japanese people believe in it whether they are consumers, company presidents or managers,' he says.

So to is his excitement in living in one of the world's more unusual and singular countries. The snow is already settling on Mount Fuji in November and the skiing season will soon be in full swing. Meanwhile there is Tokyo itself and its 100,000 restaurants of every possible shape and form to make inroads into.

Far away from the head office, Mitchinson says the Tokyo arm of JPMorgan has the feel of a small independent investment house that makes it fun to operate from.

Just to prove that it is not all work, work, work, the office is adorned by a four foot tall toy monkey adorned in an England rugby shirt.

Quite what the visiting president of an up and coming Japanese household goods manufacturer makes of that is anybody's guess.

Two steps ahead on bond street

Jonathan Platt and Sajiv Vaid,

Royal London Asset Management

by Richard Lander

The top fund manager moves ahead of his peers into new areas of opportunity. Once there, he takes advantage of the pricing anomalies on offer.

By the time the others have caught up, it may be too late. The herd moves slowly and when it finally arrives, the easy money has been made. The smart guy at the head of the pack will be halfway to another destination with some more good ideas to put into place before the others lumber over again, a day late and a dollar short.

Jonathan Platt, head of fixed interest at Royal London Asset Management, is one of those fund managers whose nose for a good angle keeps him one step ahead of his rivals. Two years ago, Platt was making hay in the secured bond market.

It was not, as he would be the first to admit, rocket science to discover an area of the fixed interest market that yielded around 50 basis points more than investment grade credits from similar (or even the same) issuers while having the near water-tight backing of property or other tangible assets. It was simply a case of being smarter than the others and being prepared to do one's own spadework. The real reason that most bond managers would not touch secured bonds was that they were not rated by the major credit rating agencies from whom they took their cues. That was fine by Platt who took his extra 50 basis points and continued to build his army of happy investors enjoying above average returns.

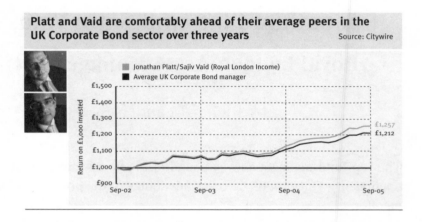

Platt and Vaid are comfortably ahead of their average peers in the UK Corporate Bond sector over three years Source: Citywire

The inevitable happened of course – other managers cottoned on to the secured bond game and as extra buying drove up prices, so yields fell along with the comparative advantage over conventional rated bonds.

This change also reflected another more general trend in the corporate bond world over the past couple of years – namely a marked flattening of spreads across the board between the highest investment grade blue chip borrowers and the less credit-worthy issues from the world of junk.

Secured bonds still play an important part in the £285 million Royal London Income Trust, which Platt runs with Sajiv Vaid, but the new rules of the fixed interest investment game mean that the two managers have had to dig deep to keep their comparative advantage over others.

But these are ideal markets for those prepared to work hard and look for new angles and it has been a very rewarding couple of years for Platt and Vaid. Performance wise, the Income Trust has continued to do well, outperforming the average fund in the UK Corporate Bond sector in the 12 month periods to August 2005 and 2004 (as the fund did in the three previous years).

The fund has also doubled in size over the last two years to about £270 million for which Platt generously gives due credit to the Royal London marketing team. 'We have seen more and more financial advisers, and particularly multi-managers, come into the fund with meaningful sums of money,' he says.

Bonding together

Platt believes that teams are important in creating the best environment for fund management. 'We are very team-oriented here. Sajiv and I lead on the income trust but we also have credit analysts and a government bond team who deliver important views on the direction on interest rates,' he says.

Six months ago that team was strengthened considerably with the arrival of Paul Rayner and Stephen Peirce from SG Asset Management to provide additional expertise on both the credit and government sides of the business.

The reason that Platt and Vaid felt they needed these extra resources was because it is becoming harder to take a company and its bonds at face value.

Traditionally, large companies with a good credit rating and with the financial attributes that got them that rating – good cashflow, a healthy balance sheet and a strong range of tangible and intangible assets – would most of the time be safe places to invest. That really is not the case any more.

Allied invasion

Take the case of Allied Domecq, pillar of the FTSE 100 index, a fine company with many and varied top international drinks brands bringing in bucket loads of cash year in year out. 'On the face of it a great company to own bonds in,' says Platt 'and hence its very slim margins over government bonds.' That was until the spring of 2005 when Allied's obvious attractions made it a target for two other conglomerates in the same business – France's Pernod Ricard, a company with a lower credit rating, and Constellation Brands of the US, whose creditworthiness was more like a Vauxhall compared with Allied's Rolls-Royce status.

Bids from lower rated companies are never good for the target but in this case, the prior examination by the Royal London team of the covenants on Allied's bonds (the copious legal conditions attached to them) forewarned them just how bad things would be.

'Allied bonds fell because the market became very concerned that if either company took over – and especially Constellation – people realised it would rank far lower in priority than the newly issued bonds,' says Vaid.

'The moral is that it is no use buying a bond because the company is big, strong and has good cashflow. You have got to look at the covenants which govern each bond.'

A fragmenting market

What really makes this so important is the increasing complexity and fragmentation of the corporate bond market and the twists and turns that get thrown up as a result.

Structured debt is the name of the game. Partly a product of the rise of management buy-outs and companies being taken into private hands with leveraged capital, structured debt is also a phenomenon that reflects companies wanting to (legitimately) make the most of the assets on their balance sheet without betting everything on red in a reckless attempt to raise money to fuel foolhardy expansion.

The days of one company, one credit rating are long gone. 'Once you bought a bond from a company and it had the same rating as another issue from the same company,' says Platt. 'Now you can buy different grades of paper with very different characteristics.'

Water sports
Platt cites as an example the British domestic water supply companies. Essentially these are monopoly businesses in each region and the very model of a cashflow generator – we all need water and we pay our bills monthly or weekly – once the expensive pipes and plant have been paid for.

CVs: Jonathan Platt and Sajiv Vaid

Jonathan Platt
Born: 21 April 1962
Career: Platt has been with RLAM for 20 years and became head of fixed interest in 1992. He runs a broad range of portfolios including the Royal London Income fund.

Sajiv Vaid
Born: 30 March 1969
Career: Vaid joined RLAM in 2001 following a stint at the Gerrard Group (1994-1997) as a trainee bond fund manager and Fuji Investments as a fully fledged manager in 1997. He co-manages the Royal London Income fund with Platt.

But it is not risk free – the government likes to keep an eye on the industry to ensure that faulty water supplies or dirty rivers do not become a vote loser. And there is also an independent industry regulator which can wrong-foot the market with pronouncements about price caps and targets for reducing pollution levels on Britain's golden beaches.

Such outside risks explain why several of the companies have taken on other businesses in order to smooth out their earnings.

'You have a choice with water companies,' says Platt. 'If you like the price of their paper but have some reservations about their core business then you can buy their AAA-rated bonds. On the other hand if you like the business itself you can get a higher yield with higher risk from a subordinated bond backed by cashflow from the water bills'

There are nuances in abundance between the different water companies and the different paper they issue and (if you will excuse the pun) this is all meat and drink to Platt and Vaid. 'It is no coincidence that some of our winners over the past 18 months have come from this part of the market,' says Vaid.

Beer monsters

There must be something about liquids and complex bond arrangements because another big presence in this part of the credit markets is the major pub chains that have sprung up in Britain over the past decade as the brewers have shed the outlets for their produce and smaller groupings have consolidated.

'This has been a real growth market and the pubs are now major issuers,' says Vaid. 'As businesses, pubs have very steady cashflows. At the same time, the huge amount of corporate activity in the sector has seen share values rise on the stock market and this has allowed the operators to leverage their balance sheets.'

Vaid cites as an example Punch Taverns, now one of Britain's largest pub operators, which has gone on an impressive pub (buying) crawl since swallowing 1,400 outlets from the Bass brewing conglomerate in December 1997.

Five major purchases since then, including a deal to take almost 3,000 pubs owned by rival Pubmaster in 2003, and plenty of smaller ones have taken Punch's estate to 8,220 outlets.

Much of this was achieved through borrowings, which were entirely

While others talk of a bubble in the credit world waiting to go pop, just as the high tech phenomenon did at the turn of the millennium, Platt is more sanguine and suggests that we had all better get used to a low yield world.

'It really is not a bubble at all but instead is a reflection of our aging populations and a shift in the global savings pattern from the first world to China and Asia. It is not something that will disappear overnight,' he maintains. High-yield bonds present some of the most glaring examples of bonds being too expensive for the risk they carry, with some bonds of this ilk being issued at spreads achieved by investment grade issuers just three years ago. Platt points to what is happening at the £144 million Royal London Sterling Extra Yield Bond fund, launched in April 2003. A hugely successful offshore fund, its intention was, and is, to augment investors' returns by, as Platt puts it, 'nipping in and out of sub-investment grade bonds'.

That is becoming more difficult 'because we are finding it much harder to find high-yield bonds that offer good long-term value'. Small wonder then that Platt's flagship Income Trust has augmented its holding of top-flight AAA bonds in recent months.

So we are entering an era of more debt, in ever more varieties, from more companies at what looks like permanently low interest rates by historic measures – and all being chased by growing numbers of yield-hungry investors.

The only shortage around is brain power and the potential to think for yourself. At times like this, it is a good job for corporate bond investors that they have people like Jonathan Platt and Sajiv Vaid around to help them.

Value virtuoso

Jens Moestrup Rasmussen,

Sparinvest Fondsmaeglerselskab

by Richard Lander

When British prime minister Tony Blair came to power he made it clear what his three priorities were: 'Education, Education, Education!'

The message from Jens Moestrup Rasmussen, head of equities at Denmark's Sparinvest Fondsmaeglerselskab, is just as definite: 'Value, Value, Value!' is the slogan he works by every day of his working life.

The big difference is that while Blair has been all talk and little action – the British education system still leaves much to be desired – Rasmussen has been exactly the opposite. He lets the numbers speak for themselves. In his four years of running the €220 million Global Value fund for Sparinvest he has established it as one of the best global equity vehicles available for retail investors in Europe.

The fund has beaten its benchmark, the MSCI World index, by a substantial margin year on year. Approaching its fourth anniversary, the fund has made an annual return of more than 13% since launch, while the MSCI index is a shade lower than where it started.

That performance was good enough to place Rasmussen 21st in the Citywire Top 100 list of European fund managers in 2005.

The Luxembourg-based fund actually has deeper roots, being essentially a mirror of a Danish retail fund, Value Aktier, which Sparinvest launched in 1997. Rasmussen and Sparinvest are both pretty obsessed with the value concept. The group is based in an old merchant's house in a rather unfashionable Copenhagen suburb rather than one of the city centre's new fashionable office blocks while the fund's motto – investing for the long term in a short-term world – rather says it all about value. It is Rasmussen's job to turn those words into something more tangible.

'We want to increase and protect the capital of our investors,' he says. 'We seek long term positive returns – not absolute return or hedge fund returns – but with long only equities in good and bad times. We hope with our hearts that at the year end we have made a positive return.' The Global Value fund did lose money in 2002, much to Rasmussen's chagrin, but it was, as he says, 'probably the worst year for equity investors since the 1930s' and the loss was less than half the downturn suffered by the MSCI World index.

Accentuate the negative

Intriguingly, Rasmussen approaches his task without any of the classic attributes or beliefs of an equities fund manager. There is more than a touch of the fixed-interest manager about his background and approach. He cut his teeth after taking a Masters in Economics at the university of Copenhagen by setting up a research department at a domestic credit rating group. His primary task was to research 70,000 unlisted companies and make an assessment on their likely solvency.

Ask a typical bond manager about what is the most important factor for them when choosing investments and they will likely tell you: "I want to know if they will pay me back!" Rasmussen feels the same way about selecting an equity.

'I like to consider the downside risk before the upside potential,' he says. 'I like to put on my negative glasses – looking at the balance sheet and seeing what lawsuits or pension liabilities lie there – and ask a company's management or investor relations people about them. Only then do I look at a company's upside potential.'

Mixed in with the bond investor approach in Rasmussen's DNA is a touch of the corporate financier. Never forget, he says, that you are buying a company rather than a piece of paper. 'You have to see things in the real world, not look at whether a company is part of an index. If we think of ourselves as a corporate finance unit of a bank, we have to ask ourselves whether we would want to buy the company,' he says.

Rasmussen's formula for successful value investing sounds almost too simple to be true. Look at a stock and determine what its intrinsic value is. If the market value is 40% or more below that, buy it.

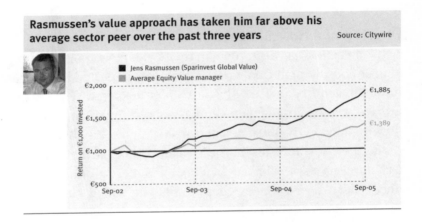

Rasmussen's value approach has taken him far above his average sector peer over the past three years   Source: Citywire

When it reaches intrinsic value, sell it. Rasmussen calls the 40% discount the 'margin of safety' and while he is quite prepared to buy a stock at that level, he really prefers an even greater margin – 60-100% or even more is the ideal.

There is of course much more to it than that – and we will return to just how you calculate a share's intrinsic value – but Rasmussen is a master at making difficult concepts sound easy to understand. He overlays two golden rules to make sure the value train runs along the right tracks.

'The first is to sell at the intrinsic value. That is part of the discipline because you don't have the downside protection at such a high price and the risk is too great. I don't care if the price then goes higher – you leave that to the other guy to worry about.

'The second key is that we do not believe in timing. We can tell you when a share is cheap but we can't tell you when it will meet intrinsic value – that's why we have lots of shares [around 100 now although the target is 110 in the portfolio].' The period it takes for a share to reach its target value can be many years – or in the fortuitous case of Safeway a matter of days – the company was bid for a mere week after Rasmussen tucked it away in his portfolio.

Once upon a time in America

Value investing has deep roots in the US, shallow roots in Europe and almost none at all in Denmark – Sparinvest imported the concept into its home country in 1997. Rasmussen is unsure why the Americans are so far ahead of the game and assumes it must have something to do with 'having the most developed stockmarket in history'.

But that is where his heroes spring from, particularly Benjamin Graham, the man who taught Warren Buffett all he knew and who once said: 'An investment operation is one which, through analysis, promises safety of principal and an adequate return. Operations not meeting these requirements are speculative.'

It has not always been so fashionable to be value-driven, Rasmussen recalls. 'I met another value legend Walter Schloss [motto: 'If a business is worth a dollar and I can buy it for 40 cents, something good may happen to me'] and others like him in the US in the late 1990s when value investing had gone out of fashion. Schloss was 85 and most value investors had become the laughing stock of the investment community. Some of them simply gave up,' he says.

While finding value stocks is very much a bottom-up process – separating the value wheat from the chaff has to be done one stock at a time – Rasmussen and the Sparinvest team make it a little easier for themselves by eliminating a vast chunk of the world's listed companies from their radar screens – those in the developing markets. As any specialist in these markets can attest, they are very much about trading off risk and growth and that is an equation that Rasmussen wants nothing to do with.

'We are quite boring here and at the same time we are focused on the downside of what we invest in,' he says. 'The worst thing that could happen is that we wake up one day and find that the government has changed and nationalised the companies that we have invested in – it is simply far too big a risk to take.'

So with the focus fully on the developed markets of the US, Japan, Australasia and Europe, Rasmussen's team combs the fundamentals

---

CV

Born: 14 September 1967
Career: Rasmussen joined Sparinvest's equity research team in 1997 focusing on Danish and Nordic equities. He began managing funds in 2000 and was appointed head of equities in 2002. Prior to joining Sparinvest he spent six years as a researcher with Købmandstandens Oplysnings Bureau.

---

databases of listed companies to see which of them can jump over their quantitative hurdles. A myriad of numbers are crunched to see whether a company has value status.

'The price/book ratio is simple but perhaps a bit too simple,' he says. 'We like enterprise multiples which compare enterprise value to earnings before items such as interest, taxes, depreciation and amortisation because it shows you how much earnings power a company has per unit of investment.'

The ratios of share price to earnings and cashflow are also examined while a low net debt to equity ratio is usually an essential requirement for a company to attain value status at Sparinvest.

'Our rule of thumb is 50% or less while the average in the MSCI World index is around 120%,' he says. 'I think it is very important that a company should be the master in its own house in case something goes wrong and it has to issue a profit warning. I am not keen at all on companies that have to go back to the bank when such circumstances arise'.

Hidden agenda

For the same reason a strong balance sheet is high on the list of criteria and the Sparinvest team spend a good deal of time searching for hidden value such as undervalued buildings or land.

The end result is a portfolio whose financial characteristics are way out of kilter with the global average, as measured by that same MSCI index. Right now in fact the net debt/equity ratio of the Sparinvest value book is just 6.6% while the price/book ratio is a mere 1.28 against the global benchmark's 3.74.

As a small operation, Sparinvest likes to whittle its value candidates down pretty quickly – as Rasmussen puts it 'we're very specialised and we want to get focused on the stuff we like to look at'.

The screening process produces first a long list of 100 possible new shares to add to the portfolio and then a short list of 20. Each of these stocks' attributes are then boiled down into a two-page internal fact-sheet. Once these have been digested, researched a little further and discussed internally over coffee and Danish pastries, the guillotine comes down again with just two or three shares emerging as being seriously worth enough examination.

'At this point what we do is what you might call traditional security analysis,' says Rasmussen. 'That involves calling the company, speaking to the investor relations people and trying to calculate the long-term earnings power of the company. We also like to look backwards and compare what the company said it was planning to do against what actually happened. For example, did the company pull itself round like the management said that it would?'

Into the unknown

As value investors all over the world have found at this point, there is not much independent research to go on. Almost by definition, value companies are not the flavour of the month and so tend not to be pushed by the investment banks. 'We do take a look at brokers' notes if there are any but generally we do it all ourselves because most of these companies are down and out and so there is little coverage by the analysts – they have simply fallen out of their research universe,' he says.

Company visits, however, are generally off the agenda because Rasmussen reckons that wandering round a turbine hall or visiting a Greenfield building site in a hard hat is generally a waste of time.

'My brother is a engineer but I'm not – he is the one who can tell a

---

INVESTMENT STRATEGY

- Classic, bottom-up value investor mixed with a good dose of conservatism
- Considers downside risk before upside potential and prefers to buy stocks which he believes are intrinsically worth 60-100% more than their market value
- Narrows his global focus by eliminating developing markets

---

good machine from a bad one. We're good at numbers, not at looking at machines, and I think you need to be a bit humble and know what you are good at and what you are not.'

Finally there is the all important valuation phase which helps compute an intrinsic value for a stock and by extension whether the current market price offers enough headroom for it to join the Global

Value portfolio. There is no magic single number here – the technique used will vary from one situation to another. One company might be an asset play where Sparinvest will attempt to gauge its intrinsic value by calculating how much it would be worth if its main parts were broken up and sold off. Another might be judged on its long-term earnings power.

Again, Rasmussen puts on his corporate banker's hat to ask himself what earnings multiple he would pay for the company if he were taking it over in the real world. 'We compare the share price with the going rate from a database of some 320,000 corporate deals – so we can know that, for example, lumber companies are bought on around seven or eight times earnings and can assign an intrinsic value based on that data.'

Slowly but surely

It's a long process and, in line with Rasmussen's conservative approach, companies are still not catapulted into the portfolio in one fell swoop.

'Smaller companies get a 0.5% share and larger companies 1%. We will then build up but for us a big stake is 2-3% – so that is why we have 100 positions in our portfolios.' But once in the portfolio, companies tend to stay in a long time – average annual turnover in the fund is a low 10%. Some of the shares can lie there as sleepers for as long as five years before Rasmussen and his team will look again at their merits for remaining in the fund.

Most other investors would have thrown in the towel long before then and sold a share that had not rewarded their faith. Rasmussen is far from arrogant and admits that mistakes do happen. Generally he sticks by his shares because he believes the Sparinvest process gets things right more often than not.

Several stocks have in the end reaped huge profits for the fund, repaying several years when little happened to them. The end of Burtonwood Brewery's life on the London Stock Exchange came in late 2005 when pub rival Wolverhampton & Dudley Breweries landed a killer blow with a takeover bid of 550p a share. Sparinvest had started buying Burtonwood shares in early 1998 at around 166p and held them throughout five years of soporific market action.

Going for a Burton

But so convinced was Sparinvest that Burtonwood's combination of loyal customers and great cashflow gave it an intrinsic value of 460p a share that it kept on buying more of the company. By the time the takeover cheque came from Wolverhampton, Sparinvest had an average buying price of just 208p a share.

Not a lot of people know that:

Rasmussen signed up for the 90 kilometre Swedish ski race, Vasa Loppet, with no prior experience in cross country skiing. After 10 painful hours he made it to the finish line – about five hours behind the winner.

If there is one factor that cuts down the average life of a share in Rasmussen's portfolio it is that its discount to intrinsic value is also recognised by a trade rival (or increasingly, a private equity player) and the company's life as a quoted entity comes to an abrupt, and for Sparinvest profitable, end.

Between 2000-2002, the fund sold 93 shares of which no fewer than 32 departed as a result of a takeover. The trend has continued since then with Burtonwood joined by such varied names as Weetabix, Grey Global and JJB Sports all challenged by real or mooted takeover approaches.

Very few stocks in the Global Value fund are listed on the US market – not because Rasmussen has any prejudice against the home of value investing but because his market-agnostic investment process simply doesn't turn up many candidates there. 'The US has been in a long- term upturn fuelled by tax reforms and consumption,' he says.

Favourite places

The converse of this is naturally that the Global Value fund is substantially overweight in Germany and Japan, countries where the economies have been in intensive care for most of the past decade.

And while it is now suddenly fashionable to talk of Japan's phoenix-like recovery, Rasmussen has been heavily overweight there since 1998 when most investors would not have touched the market there with the proverbial bargepole. 'You were able to buy global companies there at a discount and domestic ones at cheap prices,' he says.

Rasmussen still sees plenty of upside in both countries. 'Japan and Germany have the potential in their economies which will come out of solving problems for the long term – I cannot see that happening in the US,' he says.

From a wider perspective, Rasmussen acknowledges that the global balance is tilting as the supercharged economies of China and India power ahead. But even if most investors seek growth in these areas, he is certain that value will win in the longer term, as he maintains it has throughout investing history.

'There will always be value investments,' he says. 'People have different measures of success. Short-term investors like positive stories but that is only human nature. But then stocks disappoint and get sold off and become value shares.' Nor is the current value story, which succeeded the boom years of the late 1990s, about to run out of steam. It is not value stocks that have raced ahead and closed the gap on growth sectors, but the other away round according to Rasmussen.

'What has really happened is that value stocks have only been re-rated a little while growth valuations have failed dramatically. People are simply willing to pay far less for growth than they were in the days of the bubble,' he says.

It may be no surprise to learn that Rasmussen was once a marathon runner – a branch of athletics that requires dedication, stamina, patience and an eye for the finishing line many miles away.

He gave up the marathons some time ago ('twenty five kilos ago to be precise', he admits) but it looks like he will be picking up value stocks for a long time to come.

Do the right thing

Ted Scott,

F&C Asset Management

by Richard Lander

Ted Scott would prefer it if you described him as a very good fund manager who happens to run ethical funds, rather than a very good ethical fund manager.

It is an important difference and one that happened to be crystallised in July 2005 when his employers, F&C Asset Management, handed him the reins of the non-ethical UK Growth & Income fund.

Within months, Scott had underlined his credentials to mix with the best managers, green or otherwise, by vastly improving the performance of what had been a rather lacklustre vehicle – and incidentally, investing in a large number of companies that would have no chance of making it into his ethical funds. In any case, as Scott points out, it is not he who decides whether a company is acceptable to be included in the £1.75 billion Stewardship Growth fund and the £230 million Stewardship Income fund that he has run, or helped run, since joining what was then Friends Provident in 1984.

Other people decide what he can and cannot invest in and he gets on with picking the best on the acceptable list. This he has done with consistent and excellent performance which led to his award as Citywire Lipper UK Equity Income Fund Manager of the year 2005.

It was partly accident that brought Scott into ethical fund management. Having studied economics at Exeter and learned the ropes of broking in three years at Schaverien, a small private client house of the type rarely seen today, he joined Friends' fund management arm as an extra pair of hands when the first Stewardship fund was launched. 'It was a very small team then with no specific roles,' he said.

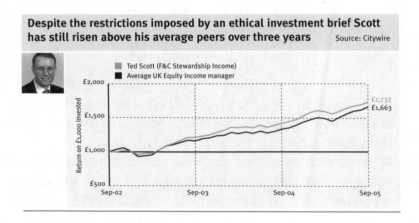

Despite the restrictions imposed by an ethical investment brief Scott has still risen above his average peers over three years Source: Citywire

Ted Scott (F&C Stewardship Income)
Average UK Equity Income manager

Return on £1,000 invested

£2,000
£1,500
£1,000
£500

£1,732
£1,663

Sep-02 Sep-03 Sep-04 Sep-05

The journey to being part of the giant F&C family, with more than £125 billion of assets under management, has come through a series of takeovers and mergers that has brought in such famous names from the fields of fund management and life assurance as London & Manchester, Ivory & Sime, UK Provident, Royal & SunAlliance and Isis into Scott's remit.

Throughout this blizzard of logos and business cards, his job description has remained the same – to look after the money of investors who want to avoid supporting companies involved in drugs, tobacco, arms, pollutants and other goods and services they feel to be ethically unsound. Ethical funds were a natural fit with Friends Provident, a life group which had Quaker roots dating back to its foundation as the Society of Friends in 1832, and had for the most part eschewed companies dealing in the most unethical sectors of the market such as tobacco and alcohol.

It was, however, a less than auspicious start to the fund which was the first in the UK and based on a series of launches in the US. Initially, the whole idea of such a fund, which at first glance threatened to compromise investors' returns through a vastly reduced universe of investments, was turned down by the Department of Trade and Industry which at that time governed such matters.

Winning over the cynics

Only once the approach was reworked, complete with a glaring wealth warning to drill home the message to investors who were probably already aware of what they were doing, was permission granted for money to be raised. Even then, sceptics in the press and the City saw it as an ultra-niche product for those who preferred their shoes to be made of canvas and their diet to be largely roughage-based.

Along with those other famously pessimistic initial sales predictions such as computers (10, according to IBM founder Thomas Watson) and mobile phones (around 600,000), most people saw the first Stewardship fund scratching its way to around £5 million.

Today Scott, as F&C's head of Stewardship funds, is responsible for more than £2 billion of ethically-run money while computers and mobiles are now in their billions.

So why is Scott reluctant to assume the ethical fund manager label? It is not because he is unethical personally – he describes his own attitude as 'moderately ethical – I'm not a member of Greenpeace but I enjoy the countryside and would prefer that it wasn't destroyed'. Principally it is because other people decide the shares that are part of his investment universe. 'Investors who choose us do so because they are ethical, so we have to have a strong, robust and thorough process for them and we invest a substantial amount of money to do this for them.' Scott says. 'We like to make the point to people that we are not just paying lip service to ethical investing.'

The route to entry into a Stewardship fund is a testing one which will take a company and its shares through two committees. The first, the committee of reference, sets out the principles of stewardship that acceptable companies have to abide to – the broad categories such as their attitude towards the environment, labour relations, fair trade, bribery and corruption.

The actual share-by-share decisions are then taken by the investment sub-committee which interprets the principles into the acceptable list which serves as Scott's investment universe.

Passing the screen test

Importantly, as Scott points out, both committees are independent and both meet regularly to assess change as events and conditions dictate. 'For example, South Africa used to be rejected on principle during the apartheid years and is now included,' he says. 'At the stock level, the investment committee has recently changed its mind about BAA, which we can no longer have in the fund given its plans to expand Heathrow and Stansted and the extra pollution that will cause.'

As if that was not enough, Scott can also call on a wide range of other resources, both in house and out of house, to know a company and its ethical credentials inside out. F&C's 14-strong team of analysts in its Government & Socially Responsible Investment (GSRI) unit engages at any one time with more than 1,000 companies in the UK and around the world on a myriad of issues ranging from animal testing to Aids and the environment.

Apart from providing the investment sub-committee with a detailed ethical assessment of any given company, the GSRI team has also become a profit centre for F&C, selling its services to outside investors who need the knowledge to cope with the mushrooming number of ethical investment laws here and abroad.

The investment universe as Scott gets to see it at the end of this exhaustive process is a very shrunken one compared with the one that nearly all his rivals can deal with. 'I have around 400 companies that I can look at in the UK and I can't invest in around 70% of the market by capitalisation,' he says.

The emphasis is inevitably on smaller and medium-cap stocks given the concentration of unethical activities in FTSE 100 stocks, particularly the miners, tobacco, drug, oil and alcohol multi-national giants which so fuel the conspiracy theories of anti-globalisation protesters.

CV

Born: 9 February 1959
Career: Scott graduated in Economics from Exeter University. He began his career at Schaverien (Private Client Stockbrokers) in 1981. He arrived at Friends Provident's asset management arm (now F&C Asset Management) in 1984. Scott joined the Stewardship team in 1987 and took overall responsibility for the Stewardship funds in 2000. He was handed F&C's UK Growth & Income fund in July 2005.

So is Scott frustrated by the strictures under which he works? Well, yes, but only up to a point and only at certain times – 2005 being a prime example. 'We have had the very strong oil price this year and at times like this you just can't keep up with the market with funds such as these,' he says. 'But you just have to shrug your shoulders and minimise the damage. I tell investors that ethical funds won't necessarily be worse than others – just different. Over the past five years we have had more good times than bad and there is no point in complaining.'

At the same time, Scott is keen to emphasise that his work only starts when the committees have stopped deliberating and that he is not by nature a committee man. 'I like to work in teams as I do here but I also like to make my own decisions and come to my own judgements. I have only got myself to blame if things go wrong,' he says.

The whole, wide world

While Scott likes to portray his investment process as a mixture of top-down and bottom-up analysis, he starts with the macro economic background as befits his university education.

'I start from the top down because I am trying to get a view of the UK economy in the context of what is happening in the global economy and world markets,' he says. 'From there we can get an idea of just what sort of stocks that we be investing in.

Scott's allocation model for equities starts by dividing up his universe into defensives, cyclicals, growth stocks and others. 'We make that decision first. For example if we feel that the economy is going to expand more than the market is expecting then we would shift the balance towards cyclicals. If not we would emphasise our defensive stocks rather more,' he says.

Much time during this part of the process is spent, head down, looking at the work of economists and strategists and hearing what they have to say.

'We have a strategy team here but I don't necessarily take the house view. I always tend to follow my own instincts because I feel closer than they are to the equities market and I know what the market is discounting,' he says. 'At the same time I have to have a feeling for the relative merits of equities as an asset class because I can also buy corporate bonds for the Income fund.'

Scott's reading takes him far and wide. He spends time reading the runes of the money markets, particularly gilts, index-linked stocks and interest rates because they can quite often be good leading indicators for the economy and the stockmarket. Outside writers he admires include James Montier and Albert Edwards of Dresdner Kleinwort Wasserstein ('Although I don't always agree with them') and the Morgan Stanley strategy team. Distilling this mass of information is hugely important for Scott's work. 'I put a lot of time and effort into getting the structure of my portfolios right. You have to get a clear view of the bigger picture,' he maintains. 'Over the past five years it has been very important to get your sectors right – you can spend far too much time picking stocks.'

The bargain basement

From the bottom-up perspective, Scott's main mission is to get stocks that have attractive valuations and (where appropriate) dividend yields relative to the rest of the market. The emphasis here is on the whole of the market – Scott and his colleague Hilary Aldridge, who specialises in small stocks, will place the companies he can invest in within the context of those he cannot touch.

The logic is simple. Just because a stock is valued attractively compared with the universe of Scott's ethical companies does not make it an immediate buy if it is wildly overvalued within the market as a whole. Familiarity with the whole of the market stood Scott in good

---

INVESTMENT STRATEGY

- Two independent committees initially scrutinise stocks and draw up a suitable list from which Scott chooses
- Scott divides his investment universe into defensives, cyclicals, growth stocks and others before deciding on any specific stock
- He prefers earnings-based valuations to alternative measures in the belief a firm's fortunes depends on what it does with its cash

---

stead when it came to taking over the unrestricted UK Growth & Income fund in 2005.

Scott's belief in relative valuations is based on three reasons. The first is that most stocks tend to trade within a 40% price/earnings valuation range which makes spotting their attractive buy and sell prices reasonably easy. 'For example we can see from our charts that Tesco has traded within a relative value range of 90-120, so it looks cheap when it reaches its prospective valuation of 90,' he says. 'Yet it has looked expensive to us over the past year – a time when the price has gone nowhere – while brokers have been saying it looks cheap,' he says. And as Scott points out, most analysts only get to see Tesco through the eyes of the supermarket sector. He wants to know whether it is good value compared with the whole of the market.

The second reason is that valuation judgements dovetail with the way Scott feels investment decisions should be made. 'It is a much better way than by looking at what is happening to share prices. Day-to-day move-ments are irrelevant,' says Scott, who subscribes to the view of famed Morgan Stanley strategist Barton Biggs that you need to be as far away as possible from the 'noise and babble of the day-to-day market'.

The third reason is the best of all – it works. 'We have used this very successfully since the inception of Stewardship,' he says. 'Richard Lowman, the funds' only other manager, followed the method and I carried on after he retired in 2000.'

Scott sticks with earnings-based valuations despite the more recent vogue for alternative yardsticks to measure a company's success, ranging from discounted cashflow to return on capital employed as well as those that eschew interest payments, depreciation and amor-tisation. 'Cashflow methods are important but earnings are more important because a company's fortunes depend on what it does with the cash. If you under invest it will destroy shareholder value. 'Yes you have to be cautious how you interpret earnings but it is more a ques-tion of how you use them,' he says. He ascribes the fetish for dividends in the past few years as a reaction to the late 1990s when companies made silly acquisitions but were penalised in the growth-fixated bull market for paying dividends. However, he says companies are now beginning to be rewarded for reinvesting their money once again, albeit more sensibly. Nevertheless, he recognises the importance for yield because, as he says: 'In the longer term dividends provide about two-thirds of total investment return.'

If the limits of ethical investing have pointed Scott's Stewardship funds towards smaller, growth stocks, that is generally fine by him – if for no other reason than that the FTSE 100 index and the larger end of the FTSE 250, scene of so much of his forbidden fruit, is very well covered by the body of company analysts that it is almost impossible to get extra information that has not been discounted by the market as a whole.

Alexandra the great

Give Scott an AIM company or one at the smaller end of the main market, however, and he will be on full alert for the hidden jewels. One of his favourites in recent times has been Alexandra, the workwear and uniforms company, which he bought for his Stewardship Income fund three years ago on a yield of almost 9%.

'We had a very good meeting with them just as the market turned. Most of the market hated textile companies at that time but we could

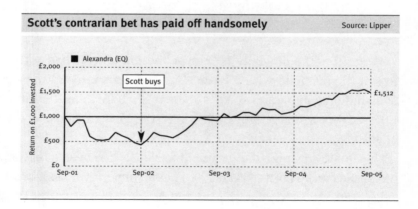

see Alexandra rationalising and outsourcing production to Morocco and the Far East while being more innovative and winning new accounts. It was going through a period of survival but the shares have doubled since we bought them and the yield has increased.'

Pumping up on barbells

And today of course we have Ted Scott, the man for all sectors rather than just Ted Scott, ethical investor. When he assumed control of the UK Growth & Income fund in the summer of 2005 he inherited a poorly performing traditional income fund that only looked at companies as potential portfolio constituents if they yielded a certain level. What he transformed the fund into was a barbell type of vehicle that generated safe income from one set of shares, particularly those from the banking or utilities sectors, and looked for growth from more dynamic shares whatever their income.

Not a lot of people know that:

Scott is mad about David Bowie. When the creator of pop personas such as Ziggy Stardust tours the UK, Scott won't settle for attending just one concert, he'll be booking tickets for as many gigs as he can.

By the time he officially took over the fund, Scott had turned over 70% of the portfolio with a large chunk of the shares in the ethically unsound oil and mining sectors such as Shell, BP and Rio Tinto.

These sectors were, after all, where the growth was and their low yields were no constraint.

The effect was immediate – the fund, which had been a bottom quartile performer in both 2003 and 2004 began to perform again while F&C sales staff reported renewed buying interest from financial advisers on the back of Scott's reputation.

Mind watching

That reputation is built on much more than the spreadsheets and stock screens that are so much of a part of Scott's work. Scott is also a keen student of behavioural finance – the psychology of investment behaviour that drives some players in the market to do irrational things. 'It adds a more human dimension to what I do and gets you away from the day-to-day emotions of the market,' Scott says.

He is particularly intrigued by such behaviour patterns as anchoring ('a share disappoints but people won't admit they are wrong and won't sell as a result') and its second cousin, loss aversion ('where investors won't sell when their shares are showing a loss and tell themselves 'I'll just hold on until it goes back up again…'').

Again he is a big fan of James Montier, who wrote the seminal book on the subject of behavioural finance, although Scott says he is less extreme in his views than Montier. 'While I am sceptical about the value of talking to large companies, Montier claims that meeting any of them is a complete waste of time because they tell you what you want to hear and you only hear what you want to hear,' he says.

You get the impression from Scott that he is a propaganda-proof zone and that no amount of corporate hype can deflect him from either his instincts about a company's worth or the results of his thorough analysis. In an age where spin is king and facts tend to be flexible in the hands of those doing the spinning, he is a useful man to have on your side.

Pulling out all the stops

Andrew Sutherland,

Standard Life Investments

by Richard Lander

Andrew Sutherland likes a challenge. Every Sunday he takes on the might of the venerable Willis organ of St Michael's Church, Linlithgow near his home to provide the musical accompaniment to the weekly service. It is a beast that takes some skill to master complete with electric bellows, two keyboards, pedals and 1,700 pipes to mimic the various instruments of the orchestra.

The challenge in his day job is to make sure that Standard Life Investments, where he is investment director of fixed interest, remains competitive with its rivals by offering the type of products that its customers demand.

Organ playing has remained pretty constant over the years – the instrument Sutherland plays first delivered a tune in 1911 – but the nature of fixed interest investment has changed enormously over the 22 years he has been with the company since graduating from Glasgow University in Music (which remains his first love) and Mathematics.

'When I started here we had a typical life assurance company credit book that featured debentures and other similar instruments. There was little credit analysis of any sort then and you chose investments if they ticked the right boxes as far as asset cover and income cover were concerned,' he says.

The bonds boom

Simple days. Life grew more complicated as investors became more sophisticated and started to request investment scenarios that offered more choice on the risk and reward scale.

At the same time, the capital markets opened to new classes of borrowers that gave investors precisely that opportunity. From emerging market governments to sub-investment grade firms seeking to make audacious and highly-risky takeovers, the markets developed across a wide credit spectrum with concomitant variations in lending risk.

Different skills were required to meet this challenge. 'We responded by building up a very good credit team. We hired people with a strong background in credit analysis and blended them in with the people who were already in place to form an extremely effective capital markets machine,' Sutherland says.

It is a challenge that Sutherland relished as it brought the once-sleepy world of fixed interest into the investment limelight. And the challenge shows no sign of going away, he reckons.

'The pace of change won't give up,' he says. 'We can see opportunities to use the core credit skills of our team in new ways. It's a process of continuous change and looks likely to remain that way.'

Despite its increasing sophistication over the last two decades, Sutherland agrees the case has to be continuously made for fixed interest investment so that it is seen as something more important than just the part of an investor's portfolio that is not allocated to equities. From this perspective, Sutherland reckons things are moving in the right direction.

'We are seeing a much greater degree of specialisation and sophistication among investors than we did say 20 years ago. Advisers are becoming much more knowledgeable about different products that can supply income generation or capital growth,' he says.

'In particular we are seeing investors who are committed to finding long-term income solutions as part of their portfolios. For example, for people who have limited income, we have developed our Higher Income fund to deliver a good income quarter after quarter.'

Demographics in the shape of an aging population – and one that finds the government increasingly less willing to take care of its long-term financial needs – is another factor on the side of the fixed-interest investment industry.

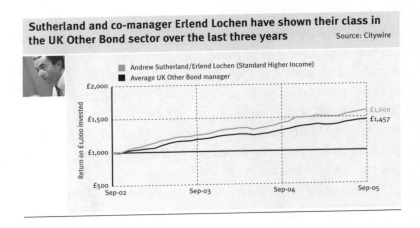

Sutherland and co-manager Erlend Lochen have shown their class in the UK Other Bond sector over the last three years   Source: Citywire

'There is evidently a growing demographic need for income regardless of what an investor has in equities. Going forward, it seems likely that we will continue to provide good products that provide growing income along with capital protection – and that is another challenge to look forward to,' he says.

Sutherland is keen to move on from the familiar question about whether people should be switching from equities into bonds, which he reckons is a sterile argument. 'It is more about having a certain amount of a portfolio in fixed interest. The most important thing is that people are now looking beyond equities to invest in other asset classes – not just fixed interest but property as well. I think that the effects of an aging population, along with continued low inflation, will keep people interested in fixed interest products.'

A decade of development

This demand for more varied products has been mirrored by the development of the Standard Life Investments range of fixed interest funds over the past 10 years aimed at retail investors. As well as his role as a head of the credit team, Sutherland runs several bond mandates including the £197 million Standard AAA Income fund and the and the £418 million Standard Corporate Bond fund. He also jointly manages the £341 million Standard Higher Income fund with Erlend Lochen and the £99 million Standard Select Income fund with Alasdair MacLean.

'In the past we started with the corporate bond fund which is now 10 years old and is our flagship product and has performed reasonably well,' Sutherland explains. 'The motive was that we had a good bond team and a strong credit process and that we could make an excellent, tax efficient vehicle for retail investors.'

The company's next step was to launch the AAA fund offering bonds issued by the most blue chip of companies and organisations. It might sound boring (and would be if launched into the low-yield environment of today) but in 1999 Sutherland and his team saw a tactical opportunity waiting to be seized.

'It was the time when there was massive bond issuance with all the telecom companies coming to tap the market. You had this incredible investment opportunity present itself in which AAA spreads on bonds issued by organisations such as the European Investment Bank ballooned out to 100 basis points over gilts [they are under 20 points today].'

It was not an easy sell. 'People's eyes glazed over but we did manage to attract a few people in there and offer a real attraction for risk averse investors,' he says.

Having plugged the gap at one end, Sutherland's next mission was to fill it at the other extreme of the risk/reward spectrum. The next step was the Higher Income fund, tapping into the growing requirement for income from retail investors that could be satisfied from the high yield end of the market – again another success but a fund that, as expected, has been volatile, especially since 2002.

Finally, the Select Income fund, launched in 2003, was an opportunistic, tactical move designed to appeal to people who wanted a step up in risk.

'We worked from the concept that spreads for companies rated BBB [higher risk than AAAs but still investment grade] were very attractive – and we also knew that when interest rates rose, these spreads would tend to come down,' he said.

CV

Born: 4 January 1959
Career: Sutherland joined Standard Life as a trainee in 1980. Within three years he was working as an analyst and in 1984 took responsibility for fixed interest segregated pension funds. He was subsequently appointed investment director of the group's specialist investment division, Standard Life Investments, on its creation in 1998. He runs a range of bond mandates including the Standard Corporate Bond fund and the Standard AAA Income fund. He also jointy manages the Standard Higher Income and Standard Select Income funds.

The economic backdrop also played a part – the economy remained strong and inflation was under control, while companies rated BBB were improving and getting their balance sheets in order. 'Again we were just responding to what the market was telling us was going on and what investors were telling us that they wanted to see from us,' he says.

Like the painting of the Forth Road bridge a couple of miles away from Standard Life Investments' Edinburgh headquarters, getting your bond range in order is an exercise that is never quite done.

The team at Standard Life Investments has other bond funds on the slipway including a global index linked fund and recently launched the Ethical Corporate Bond fund which invests in investment grade corporate bonds and other interest bearing securities from screened UK, European and US companies. 'I think this will get a great deal of interest from charities because Standard Life Investments has a proven ethical capability in both equities and bonds,' he says.

Zooming in on credit

However, is this not all a desperate attempt to keep investors looking at fixed interest at a time when low yields and thin spreads have stagnated the waters? Yes, but only up to a point, concedes Sutherland.

Not a lot of people know that:

Sutherland has a passion for The Diamonds – that's Airdrie United FC rather than the rocks, although any loyal fan will tell you the team is undoubtedly one of Scotland's gems.

'Low interest rates and stable growth means we'll see government bond yields range-bound for a while. The last two years have been really boring for gilts because we have seen the interest rate cycle moving between highs of 6% and lows of 4% – compare that with the range of between 17% and 8% that we saw in the first half of the 1980s.'

But that continuing backdrop for gilts has several implications for credit, according to Sutherland. 'As long as we have this low yield environment, it puts a lot of pressure on investors with yield targets to look closely at credit – especially in Europe,' he says.

'We have already seen that in the US where the biggest driver for high yield bonds is the state of the US Treasury market. In the end it becomes an investor preference argument rather than a credit argument.'

And if it is yield that investors are chasing, Sutherland's task becomes subtly different – as he puts it 'to avoid idiosyncratic negative risk' – or to guide investors around the 10% of the market that he reckons has blow-up potential.

Indeed 2005 became a microcosm of the way that the fixed interest market is heading – one in which company by company credit analysis has come to the fore as varied dangers threaten individual balance sheets, ranging from pension fund worries to leveraged buyouts (which immediately transform even AAA debt into high-yield junk) and industry specific slumps, as seen in the car and retail sectors.

'Things looked quite gloomy at the start of 2005 with the prospect of rising interest rates driving yields higher. There was also a huge amount of leverage in hedge funds and we had both Ford and General Motors saw their credit ratings blow up,' says Sutherland.

In the end things turned out to be better than expected. 'The credit market absorbed all of that – Ford and GM were downgraded and BBB bonds moved up by just 20 basis points. It was our job to avoid any blow ups and then look for good opportunities to buy in,' he says.

Again, Sutherland has seized the moment to try to develop Standard Life Investment's fixed interest resources to cope with the new environment. 'We developed the credit process here, adding resources and focusing on stock selection,' he says. 'For example when worries developed over B&Q in the DIY sector, we saw a large drop in the high yield bonds issued by its rival Focus. We had seen this coming and had sold Focus before B&Q happened and we would very much hope that we can buy the bonds back at cheaper levels.'

Sutherland says the company's investment process is 'one that doesn't start with either sector allocation or specific stock selections – it's a multi-level process to which each team member brings different skills.' However, with the nature of the market changing, more firepower is now being put on credit analysis and stockpicking by sector specialists.

The matrix reloaded

Despite the team's expansion in recent years, Sutherland recognises that resources will always be finite, which is why he oversaw the development of a complex credit matrix screening tool that seeks to build an overall picture of a company's credit prospects from 15 different factors. 'We look at things like equity volatility, financial ratios, the prospects for a company's shares and so on. It's the changes in each of these that are crucial,' he says.

Experience is a great, if sometimes cruel, teacher and the credit matrix has been continually revised and refined in the light of what has happened in the past. Worldcom, the giant US telecoms group that went spectacularly bankrupt through a mixture of over ambition, corporate greed and plain larceny, provided many lessons for the Standard Life Investments team.

'We had Worldcom in the portfolio and we really didn't enjoy it very much,' says Sutherland with a delightful degree of understatement. 'But after it happened the team devised a range of factors that could serve as early warning signals for the next time this happened.' These included revisions that get made to a company's accounts, less-than wise mergers and acquisitions proposals and corporate governance issues such as pension schemes that threaten to overwhelm a company's financial health in the future.

The revised matrix paid huge dividends when it alerted Sutherland

and his team to what was happening at Parmalat, the Italian food giant where huge sums of money mysteriously disappeared and sent the company's bonds plunging.

'With Parmalat the matrix score fell sharply on such criteria as the financials, equity volatility and corporate governance,' Sutherland explains. 'We really didn't like the fundamental factors either where we saw a marked lack of communication from the company.

INVESTMENT STRATEGY

- Combines a top-down approach to maximise the investment picture with an increasing focus on stock-specific indicators
- Employs a complex credit matrix screening tool which alerts the team to potential risks surrounding a company's development
- Uses the group's presence in the stockmarket to secure key company meetings senior executives

---

'The end result was that we avoided Parmalat and our European funds hugely outperformed the index. The system worked in a very similar way with the telecom sector – the matrix told us that the yield that the bonds in this sector were paying would not be high enough to justify the risk – so we avoided them as well,' he says.

Size matters

Standard Life's presence in the UK stockmarket as a massive equities investor also provides invaluable intelligence for the credit team. Company meetings are co-hosted by both sides of the business and are held under strict Standard Life Investments rules that mean company directors have to leave their glossy presentations back in the head office and submit themselves to a lengthy question and answer session.

'We are very lucky to have access to these meetings because our group's power in the stockmarket means that we get to see the chief executive officer and the finance director rather than the head of treasury or the investor relations person,' says Sutherland.

Corralling a few board level directors without even their Powerpoint presentations to defend themselves is a sport that Sutherland obviously enjoys. 'It's great to see their body language and see their animal spirits rising as they talk about what M&A activities they might get up to,' he says. 'You can gauge how much shareholder pressure they are under and you can see how committed they are to maintaining their dividends or keeping their credit rating intact.'

Different perspectives

The meetings may be held jointly but the conclusions drawn by the two sides of the asset management business can be quite different. 'It is often the case that the equities team will like the look of a company and we take the opposite view. For example when Marks & Spencer came to see us, we were lucky enough to have on our team Alasdair MacLean who had been hired by Philip Green to have a look at their books before he was contemplating making a bid for the company.

'The equities team held out great hopes for a leveraged takeover bid that would send the share price soaring while we knew it would hurt the bonds. So when the shares rose they made a lot of money and we avoided a loss – it was just a shame really that we couldn't have gone short of the bonds,' he says.

Lloyds TSB provoked the same split opinion, only the other way round this time. 'They are a very well rated bank and good for us – no overseas exposure to go wrong and a safe, if boring, story. But from an equity point of view the shares are simply not exciting.'

With so much emphasis on company-by-company analysis in today's fixed interest market, does Sutherland – a top-down, big picture sort of guy – consider himself to be an endangered species whose role will diminish as he gets surrounded by increasing numbers of very smart rocket scientists?

He admits that nobody in asset management can take anything for granted, but is probably more aware than most of his peers of the need for the financial equivalent of permanent revolution.

'Part of the problem going forward is to find different ways and means to outperform,' he says. 'So if it is not immediately there in the bond market itself you have to look at other ways such as structured credit where we use a portfolio of credit derivatives to get returns for investors with different levels of risks.'

A dynamic future

Sutherland sees his future as likely to be one of developing new products and managing them successfully. This is already beginning to happen at Standard Life Investments where much time and money has been spent developing what are known as liability driven investment solutions for pension funds which try to take a more dynamic approach to producing the returns that such funds need over periods of time as different sized cohorts of workers take retirement.

This may all sound pretty complex and a million miles away from selecting debentures that paid steady interest to pay out to life insurance policyholders. Sutherland takes it all in his stride. That is the way that the market is going and that is what investors, who pay his wages at the end of the day, are demanding. And better also, surely, that the fixed interest market is attracting new talent and innovation to produce new products and services.

In any case, it is all pretty straightforward compared with playing the Willis organ in St Michael's Church, Linlithgow every Sunday.

136

Index

About Citywire

Citywire is one of Europe's most innovative and fast-growing financial information and publishing groups.

Founded in 1999, Citywire has quickly established a reputation for incisive coverage and analysis of retail investment funds and equities markets, combining in-depth data with high-class journalism. The leading quality of its journalism was acknowledged in 2005 when the company scooped the Investment Management Association Team Award for Excellence in Investment Writing.

Citywire has won particular acclaim for its unique Fund Manager Ratings which track the personal performance records of more than 3,000 retail, life and pension fund managers across Europe.

Citywire also publishes news, data and analysis in a wide variety of formats for professional and private investors. British investors are served by the website www.citywire.co.uk as well as *Citywire Funds Insider* magazine which is read monthly by more than 6,500 leading investment advisers. The intermediary market is served by *New Model Adviser* magazine which turns weekly in January 2006.

In Europe, Citywire publishes *Citywire Fund Manager International*, sent to more than 3,000 fund selectors across the continent, and the www.citywire-fmi.com website.

Citywire also organises frequent events which bring together leading players from across Europe's fund management and advice community and publishes a wide range of books on subjects ranging from fund management to personal finance.

Citywire's success attracted the attention of Reuters, the world's leading financial information group, which bought a 25% stake in 2001.